Freak Babylon

An Illustrated History Of Teratology & Freakshows

Freak Babylon

Jack Hunter

ISBN 978-1-84068-160-4

First published 2005 by The Glitterbooks of London

This revised edition published 2010 by Creation Books

www.creationbooks.com

Copyright © Jack Hunter

All world rights reserved

Parts of this book first appeared in *Inside Teradome* (Creation Books, 1995)

contents

ONE:
TERADOME

A History of Monsters • Origins of the Freakshow

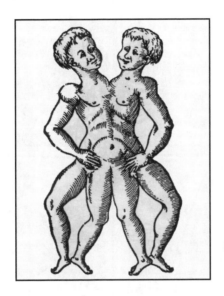

Man has always distorted his world. In the skies and the sea and far places, he has always imagined monsters and demons, mythological beasts and misshapen men. In his religions, he has conceived a weird descent of man from god and demi-god, from human folly and divine incest. Particularly, he has invented man-beasts to haunt himself, lexicons of dead souls recording hellish hybrids – minotaurs and mermen, goat-boys and gorgons, sirens and centipede-men, subterranean or amphibious cults spawned in profane antediluvian nuptial chambers. He has made half-real the terrors of his nightmares.

In classical times, Greek legends and travellers' tales peopled the earth with fantastic creatures. Heroes rode on winged horses to the rescue of maidens, killing dragons on the way. Voyagers were tempted by the deathly love and chanting of sirens. There were whole races of freakish men, some with faces sunk in their chests, others with a single foot so large it could shade them from the sun when they were not hopping upon it. From the most primitive cave-drawings, through to the medieval demonography and

infernal visions of Bosch and Grünewald and beyond, the dreams – and fears – of mankind created a phantasmagoric zoo of weird beings, the walking demons of a Hell on Earth.

Until the dawn of rationalism in the 18th century, and the beginning of classification for all species, there was little or no scientific method to distinguish between the fable and the fact. Commentators as diverse as Homer, Herodotus, Ktesias, Megasthenes, Pliny, Aristotle (who coined the term *lusus naturae*, 'jokes of nature'), through to Albrecht Dürer and Sebastian Brant with woodcuts of eight-legged sows and other monstrous births, Hartmann Schedel in his *Liber Chronicarum* (1493), Grien in the *Büch Granatapfel* (1511), Alhazred in the *Necronomicon*, Pontoppidan, Olaus Magnus in his *Historia De Gentibus Septentrionalibus* (1555), Julius Obsequens' *Des Prodiges* (1555), André Thevet in *La Cosmographie Universelle*, Pierre Boaistuau in his *Histoires Prodigieuses* (1560), Ambroise Paré in his *Animals, Monsters And Prodigies* (1573), Lycosthenes' *Prodigiorum Ac Ostentorum Chronicon*, Jacob Rueff in his *De Conceptu Et Generatione Homines* (1587), Schenck von Grafenberg in his *Monstrorum Historia* (1609), Fortunius Licetus in his *De Monstris* (1616), and Ulisse Aldrovandi in his *Monstrorum Historia* (1642), had clouded the boundaries of myth and reality almost beyond recognition. Gaspar Schott's *Miscellanea Curiosa Medica Physica* (1662) even contains instructions on how to make infants into freaks by witch-like artifice. Human monsters were otherwise attributed to the wrath of God, or punishment for the sins of sodomy (cf. Paracelsus' *De Animalibus Natis Ex Sodomia* [1493]). Paré's list of alleged causes of human monsters still reflect this superstitious viewpoint nearly a century later:

"The first is the glory of God. The second, His wrath. The third, too great a quantity of semen. The fourth, too small a quantity. The fifth, imagination. The sixth, the narrowness or smallness of the womb. The seventh, the unbecoming sitting position of the mother, who, while pregnant, remains seated too long with her thighs crossed or pressed against her stomach. The eighth, by a fall or blows struck against the stomach of the mother during pregnancy. The ninth, by hereditary or accidental illness. The tenth, by the rotting or corruption of the semen. The eleventh, by the mingling or mixture of seed. The twelfth, by the artifice of wandering beggars. The thirteenth, by demons or devils."

The first steps toward a clearer picture came from France. C. L. L. de Buffon, in his *Varieties Of The Human Species, Of Monsters* (1749), declared a new dictum which would be followed by most of his immediate successors in identifying types of human anomaly:

"All possible monsters can be reduced to three categories: the first is that of monsters by addition, *the second, monsters* by omission, *and the third, those that are such* by reason of the reversal or wrong positioning of parts."

Upon these general ground-rules, a history of human teratology would be founded.

C. E. Hoppius' *Anthropomorphia* (1760) was an early attempt to trace an evolution of beast into man; then in 1775, Regnault published his *Freaks Of Nature* (subtitled *A Collection Of The Principal Monstrosities Produced By Nature In The Animal World*). This was a collection of forty plates, drawings of 'freaks' which were all amazingly true to life. The collection was diluted only by the inclusion of a number of specimens from the animal kingdom, such as a cyclopian cat. Meanwhile various non-scientific accounts were also starting to appear, autobiographical texts such as William Hay's *Deformity:*

An Essay (1755), and Joseph Boruwlaski's *Memoirs Of A Polish Dwarf* (1788)[1].

A more exact and specific science of teratolgy was ushered in by Haller's *De Monstris*; this was the start of a period which would also see the publication of two milestones in the field: *Anatomical Philosophy* (1822) by Etienne Geoffroy Saint-Hilaire, and *Treatise On Teratology* (1837) by Isodore Geoffroy Saint-Hilaire. J. G. Milligan's *Curiosities Of Medical Experience* appeared in 1839, and at around this same time F.-E. Guerin published his encyclopaedic, 14-volume *Illustrated Dictionary Of Natural History And The Phenomena Of Nature*.

The later 19th, and early 20th centuries, would see a veritable deluge of books and treatises on human anomalies; the blood-gates had opened on the second Golden Age of Monsters. France was still at the heart, its medical bookshops filled with such tomes as Camille Dareste's *Research Into The Artificial Production Of Monstrosities*, Edward J. Wood's *Giants And Dwarfs* (1868, an early 'showbusiness' account), Lancereaux' *Atlas Of Pathological Deformity* (1871), John Davenport's *Curiositatis Eroticae Physioligiae* (1875), Jules Guérin's *Research Into Deformities* (1880), E. Martin's *History Of Monsters From Antiquity To The Present Day* (1880), Charcot and Richer's *The Deformed And The Diseased In Art*, Paul Moreau's *Fous Et Bouffons* (1885), Cordier's *Monsters In Legend And In Nature* (1890), Guinard's *Summary Of Teratology*, Blanc's *Anomalies Of Man And Mammals* (1893), George M. Gould and Walter L. Pyles' *Anomalies And Curiosities Of Medicine* (1896), *ad infinitum*. At the same time, the theatres, circuses and sideshows were brimming with live exhibits from across the globe; it seemed that the public could not get enough of them.

Although this mad passion for real 'monsters' abated somewhat with the turn of the century, with sideshows fading in popularity as cinema developed its own fantastic themes and attractions, textbooks continued to appear regularly until the '30s; most notable amongst them being Chauvin's *Summary Of Teratology* (1920), Dr. Dubreuil-Chambardel's *Variations Of The Human Body* (1925), Lesbre's *Treatise On Teratology* (1927), C. J. S. Thompson's *Mystery And Lore Of Monsters* (1930), and Binet-Sanglé's *Ancestors Of Man* (1931). One year after this, across the world in America, Tod Browning's misunderstood "horror" film *Freaks* was released to almost universal revulsion; it seemed that the public's appetite for human anomalies had, finally, reached saturation point.

The 'freakshow' itself – in other words the recognition, treatment and display of human anomalies as special beings (whether for better or for worse) – is an institution which actually dates back in one form or another to the beginnings of recorded history, in every civilization across the world. In King Assurbanipal's library in Nineveh, a tablet was found and deciphered which describes an array of recognizable human monsters; both the Assyrians and Babylonians (c.2800 BC) used anomalies to make predictions. Fetomancy involved telling the future from aborted foetuses, while teratoscopy was the art of divination from deformed births.[2] The Egyptians made gods of dwarfs, such as Bes, Ita, and Ptah, and set their images on altars.[3] Mutu, the two-headed god, was worshipped in temples consecrated to his name, as were the jackal-headed Anubis and ibis-headed Thoth. So great was their passion for dwarfs that many children were deliberately deformed, made to grow up confined in boxes or with limbs bound into distorted shapes. Pnumhotpu, a misshapen dwarf who became master of the Pharaoh's wardrobe, was acclaimed by poets and immortalized by court sculptors; even the corpse of Tutankhamen was floated across the waters of death on a raft crewed by naked achondroplasic dwarfs. One of the first dwarf court jesters was also an Egyptian, named Danga (c.2600 BC); equally renowned was Bahalul, jester to the Persian Caliph Haroun-al-Rashid.

The Greeks deified hermaphrodites and other androgynous creatures, though reputedly scorned hunchbacks and cripples; the Spartans left all their deformed offspring out to perish; the Romans, on the other hand, derived the utmost pleasure from all manner of malformed beings – as befits the originators of the circus. Like the Egyptians before them, they were not averse to creating freaks by the purposeful twisting and dislocation of infant bodies. Nero, Tiberius, Caligula and the other megalomaniac emperors were constantly surrounded by retinues of strange anomalies; Domitian sent his private legion of achondroplasic dwarf-gladiators into the arena to do battle with ferocious Amazon women, and it is reported that the finest ladies of Rome would wait in hiding to watch these naked warriors train, so great was the phallic power accredited to dwarfs (who could be bought in a special market, the *Forum Morionium*). Augustus Caesar had a pet dwarf named Lucius. Heliogabalus, maddest of them all, adored the company of his dwarfs, and gave them the power over life and death. Sulla went so far as to gather a bizarre harem of female hunchbacks, dwarfs, cripples, and the limbless, all of whom he lusted after without surcease; likewise Julia, grand-daughter of Augustus, who assembled a similar throng of gargoyles for the sole aim of pleasuring her in unparalleled orgies of sexual gratification and cruelty. Hsuan Tsany, emperor of old China, was said to have been madly in love with a two-headed courtesan, who embraced and caressed him with her four arms. Chinese women were also ritually subjected to foot-binding, a practice which stunted and rounded their feet so they might be used as pseudo-vaginas by their masters.

Human anomalies had something of a worse time with the rise of Christianity; in the Middle Ages, Christians persecuted and burnt at the stake anything and everything which they feared or did not understand, including cats and other animals, women and 'witches', gypsies, even books. In this genocidal environment, 'monsters' had no chance; their twisted bodies were sure sign that they were the progeny of Satan. Even normal twins were roasted as things of evil. Not until the rise of Nazism – with which Christianity bears closest comparison – in the 20th century would there be such an exterminating purge declared on the physically impaired or mentally retarded.

The Renaissance signalled a general return to favour for anomalies, and this period was soon to establish itself as the second 'golden age' of monsters. Astronomer Tycho Brahe, for one, relied exclusively on the prognostications of his dwarf advisor, Zep. The courts of Europe thronged with dwarfs and hunchbacks, giants, pinheads, and the limbless, becoming veritable menageries. Often used as executioners, dwarfs payed for the privileges of court by having their tongues cut out and eardrums run through with hot wires lest they repeat state secrets. The Medicis had a special 'dwarf-pit' constructed, in which naked male and female achondroplases were set to fornication, fellation and sodomy for the voyeuristic delight of the officials; the twisted servitors of Philip II, who sought out dwarfs both male and female for his pleasures, are immortalized on the façade of the Prado; Louis II of Bavaria collected madmen; while King Adolphus Frederick of Sweden kept a harem of amputee lovers. Other dwarf-collectors included King Sigismund-Augustus of Poland, the Roman Cardinal Vitelli – who had a retinue of 39 specimens – and Peter the Great, who in 1710 threw a wedding banquet for no less than 70. Catherine the Great, conversely, hankered after giants. Eventually disillusioned by their poor bedroom performances, she resorted to copulating with stallions and was reputedly killed by one such beast when it burst from harness.

Victor Hugo tells of James II and his monster-factories, where normal people were butchered and mutilated to be churned out as deformed playthings, or beggars, to order. Sculptors in human flesh held sway, and charlatans could make a fortune selling ointments to promote dwarfism or other lucrative handicaps in infants.

Chiefs in this field were the *Dacianos* (later referred to as *Comprachicos* ['child-buyers'] by Hugo in his novel *L'Homme Qui Rit*), a nomadic and mendicant sect descended from migrant Hindustani tribesmen. The manufacture of cripples and freaks was their stock-in-trade. Dr Carlos Garcia in his *La Desordenada De Los Bienos Agenos* (1619) confirms: *"The Dacianos kidnap young children and cripple and disfigure them so they may be sold to beggars and blind men."* A common trick was to slash a child's mouth open from ear to ear, giving him the permanent grin of a clown. Such mutilations were also commonplace in China and India, where priests earned a living as travelling eunuch-makers. Castration was also practised in Europe to produce young boy sopranos, *castrati* whose vocal range could not be matched by women. Even in England, court tradition called for the cutting of a man's larynx to turn him into a human cock whose hideous crowing marked the passage of night.

This mania for human anomalies scarcely abated with the dawn of the 18th and 19th centuries. Jan Bleu opened his legendary *House Of Monsters* in Amsterdam; the French Royal Court was scandalized by the sexual exploits and bizarre tastes of Petit-Pépin, a phocomelian midget whose image appears in Regnault's *Freaks Of Nature*; the Duke of Lorraine, Stanislas Leczinski, favoured his hideous midget Nicholas Ferry above all other, nick-naming him 'Baby' and indulging his murderous assaults on dogs and the other court dwarfs alike; Frederick I collected giants – dead or alive; Frederick II followed suit, and went so far as to create a regiment of them – in doing so bankrupting the treasury.

One of the last famous English dwarfs in private service was 'Nanibus', the outlandishly-caparisoned retainer of the eccentric William Beckford, author of the Gothic masterpiece *Vathek*. Meanwhile, the progress

er. Bosche Inuent.

Aux Quatre Vents

l dat op den blauwen trughelsack, gheerne leeft
jaet meest al Cruepele, op beyde syden,

Daerom den Cruepelen Bisschop, veel dienaers heeft,
Die om een vette proue, den rechten ghanck myden

P.T. Barnum and Tom Thumb

of medical research had engendered a proliferation of 'resurrectionists' – professional grave-robbers, employed by the likes of surgeon *extraordinaire* John Hunter ("the father of British surgery") to retrieve the finest teratological specimens fresh from the earth. Hunter, author of *On Monsters* (1775), was renowned not only for his extensive collection of human skulls and other exotica, but also for the notorious iron melting-pot in which he boiled away the meat and fat from anomalous human bones.

Another Englishman, Sergeant-Major Philip Ashby, born in 1742, was reputedly responsible for establishing the format of the "Three-Ring" circus; he also inaugurated the sideshow, setting up exhibitions of both human and animal anomalies as well as ghoulish artefacts such as the guillotine (complete with wax heads). Then, across the Atlantic, came the greatest showman of them all, the man who would make the freakshow a way of life – Phineas Taylor Barnum (1810-91).

Barnum founded his American Museum in 1841, a New York establishment boasting many 'freak' attractions. From this base, he was to set up his fabled travelling circus. Barnum's first major attraction was the legendary midget, Tom Thumb. Born Charles S. Stratton in Bridgeport, Connecticut, in 1838, this tiny human being was discovered by Barnum, taken to New York and introduced as General Tom Thumb from England. Tom soon became world-famous, and also incredibly wealthy (he started to collect the diamonds and other riches showered on him by high society), even entering a scandalous affair with the actress Cora Pearl. He eventually married the midget Lavinia Warren in 1863; the wedding was the event of the social season, with gifts from the likes of the Rockefellers, the Vanderbilts, and even President Lincoln, being put on display by Barnum. Tom Thumb retired a very rich man, aged 20. When Barnum made some bad investments, Tom came out of retirement to bail him out, making himself another small fortune – despite having grown to nearly 3 feet tall – in the process. Tom Thumb died in 1883, but the global mania for freakshows and outlandish theatricals raged on for the rest of the century.

This cult of deformity culminated in the giant Barnum and Bailey shows in London in 1887 and Paris in 1901, in which a massive retinue of "living phenomena and human prodigies" was advertised and displayed, comprised of both genuine anomalies and music-hall attractions alike. The full billing for Paris read as follows:

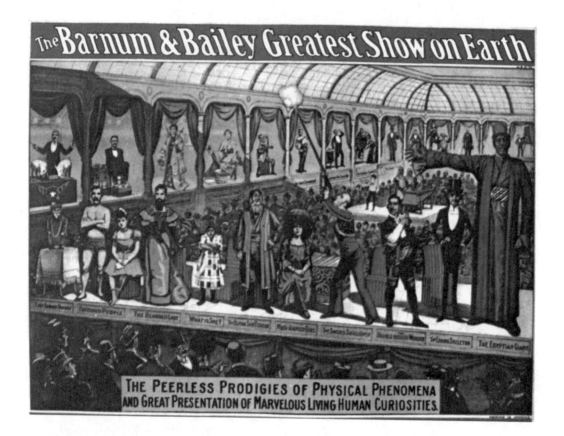

BARNUM AND BAILEY
Giant American Museum of Human Prodigies and Phenomena
An extraordinary and unique collection of bizarre human beings

GIANTS, DWARFS, PERFORMERS
who work without hands and others who support themselves without feet. Human beings endowed by nature with limbs that others do not possess. Others deprived by nature.

A happy colony of privileged beings who live, work, suffer and enjoy all the feelings common to mortals, who are in some cases happier than their fellow-men more favoured by nature.

These phenomena draw high salaries, make good investments, and many of these strange beings depicted on our posters and exhibited on our stages ought to be envied rather than pitied by all.

The Japanese Conjuress

MISS SHIMAKURI is one of the very rare feminine exponents of the art of the famous Robert Houdini. However, her conjuring tricks and feats of prestidigitation are quite different from those of that master; they have an Oriental flavour that sometimes borders on occultism. This is more than skill; it is sorcery.

The Microscopic Japanese Juggler

An atom of humanity. A fragment of Oriental grace, and expert in the art of juggling.

The Hercules With The Elastic Chest

MASTER HERMAN is gifted with an astonishing power. Merely by breathing, that is to say, by the expansive power of his lungs, he breaks the solid steel chains and strong iron rings that are bound round his chest.

The Poodle Man

JO-JO is a rare example of the whims of nature: an unbelievable and insoluble mystery. He seems to combine everything that is shocking and unpleasant. The most perceptive mind in the head of a dog. The mouth of a dog speaking four languages. This young Russian is known as the Poodle-Man because of the long, silky hair that covers his face, eyes, nose, ears, chin, and neck. Several names have been given to him, but the 'Poodle-Man' seems to be the most appropriate, for his physiognomy most resembles this breed of dog.

The Sword Swallower

MISS CLIFFORD must surely be the oddest and most original performer ever seen. The capacity of her throat amazes everyone. She puts big, sharp swords, daggers and bayonets into her mouth and pushes them gently down until no more than the hilt can be seen. She completes these extraordinary feats by swallowing gold and silver wrist-watches, and other indigestible objects.

The Fry Brothers

are the most entertaining performers. They play the 'Marimba', a very resonant musical instrument that has never been mentioned in musical history and is, nevertheless, widely played among the natives of Guatemala and the South American countries.

From left to right: Laloo, Master Herman, James Coffey, James Morris, Jo-Jo.

From left to right: Annie Jones, Annie Howard, Lia May, unknown giant, unknown tattooed man, and The Girl With The Mossy Hair.

The Man With The Ostrich Stomach

ALFONSO is known as the 'African Phenomenon' because of his enigmatic powers of swallowing and digestion. He is an absolutely exceptional human being. He chews up glass, pebbles, and other hard substances, swallows nails and sharp, pointed sheets of metal; he eats cotton wool for his second course and ordinary soap for his hors d'oeuvres, washing down this strange menu with frequent mouthfuls of petrol and ammonia.

The Magnetic Woman

MISS ZOLINO, a young lady of striking beauty, has some most unusual talents. In particular, we should mention the sword-climbing. This exercise consists in climbing barefoot up and down a ladder with steps made of razor-sharp swords; in addition, she has extraordinary magnetic qualities which give her unheard-of strength, which confounds the combined efforts of ten strong men.

The Leopard Girl

This remarkable little girl was born to an American negress in the State of Louisiana. She presents one of the greatest oddities that nature, in her peculiar vagaries, can produce, that is to say, a skin of two distinct colours. Her skin, which should properly be black all over, has large white patches rather like piebald horses, leopards' skin, or tortoise-shell, or certain kinds of marble.

The Albino

ROB ROY gives the strangest performances in the world. Medical science can find no explanation for them. He is a perfect example of the human variety known as 'Albinos'; in addition, he has the rare ability to dislocate every bone in his body.

The Armless Man

CHARLES TRIPP is a phenomenon. He was born without arms and, in default of hands, uses his feet so cleverly that he can even thread needles; he writes superbly, uses a penknife to sharpen his pens or pencils, and is, in a word, as skilful with his feet as other people are with their hands.

The Midget

QUEEN MAB. A pretty, microscopic little person, perfectly formed in every respect, except in size, she weighs only 19 lb 13 oz and is only 22" tall. She speaks several languages fluently and has a great many accomplishments, doubly remarkable in such a small person. She so much resembles a living doll that children often want to take her home with them to play with her.

The Tattooed Man

FRANK HAYES has his whole body completely tattooed with a thousand designs in Indian ink. These tattoos, which are very fine, and very artistically executed, represent strange figures, flowers, birds, and wild animals. They are like the tattoos cannibals used to inflict on their victims, and convey an idea of the customs of primitive peoples.

The Skeleton Dandy

Certainly the thinnest man in the world, a real skeleton. He is the world champion for light weight in adults; his legs and arms are real pins, and his body looks like an X-ray photograph. Nothing but skin and bones!

The Woman With Long Hair

MISS MABEL, a pretty young American, has phenomenally long and beautiful hair, which covers the floor when she stands upright.

Tomasso, The Human Pincushion

This strange man has a remarkable power which has hitherto been observed only in the Fakirs of the East. He sticks all kind of pointed instruments into his skin. One of the most astounding tricks in his repertoire consists in allowing a threaded needle to be passed through his naked arm by a member of the audience.

The Lightning Calculator

SOL STONE is a most peculiar man who has a miraculous gift for mathematics. His propensities and his conception of numbers defy description. He adds up enormous columns of figures with unbelievable speed, and takes no more than a second to make calculations that would take trained mathematicians whole hours.

The Man With The Unbreakable Head

BILLY WELLS certainly has the most extraordinary skull. This remarkable man places enormous blocks of granite on his head and holds them there with his own hands, while a member of the audience beats the granite with a blacksmith's hammer, until the block falls to pieces.

The Mastodon Man

One of the biggest men ever seen; his bulk, corpulence, and weight are enormous. There may possibly have been taller men, but surely none whose all-over measurements were as phenomenal as this.

The Telescope Man

This exhibit is a young man born in America. He has an exceptionally strong constitution. But his chief distinction, which has earned him a place in this brotherhood of exceptional human beings, is his ability to lengthen or shorten his spinal column at will. In so doing, he considerably increases or decreases his height. This oddity, due to anatomical reasons that would take too long to explain here, can be compared to the reptiles' ability to stretch and contort themselves.

The Rubber Man

JAMES MORRIS is an unparalleled phenomenon. His skin is as elastic as rubber, and can stretch enormously. The skin on his nose, cheeks, arms, chest and legs can be stretched 20" away from his body, while he can cover his whole face with the skin of his chin and neck.

The Girl With The Mossy Hair

is a delightful young person. She has a magnificent head of hair which, unlike that of most girls, looks like a tuft of moss, so very thick that it stands straight up on her head like a spear.

The Bearded Woman

MISS ANNIE JONES is another example of the whims of nature. She is an extremely pretty person, but has a long beard. She also has very beautiful hair: it is 4' 10" long. This young lady is indeed an interesting figure and has been the subject of scientific research.

The Armless Japanese Girl

MISS OGURI, a native of Japan, is a most prepossessing person. Like her colleague, Mr. Charles Tripp, she has no arms, but like him she has learned to use her feet with amazing skill. Few people could do with their hands what this clever, though incomplete, Japanese girl does with her feet.

Some of these acts may seem less than remarkable, but the crowds came nonetheless. As Barnum himself proclaimed:

"If my puffing was more persistent, my advertising more audacious, my posters more glaring, my picture more exaggerated, my flags more patriotic and my transparencies more brilliant than they would have been under the management of my neighbours, it was not because I had less scruple than they, but more energy, far more ingenuity, and a better foundation for such promises."

Though Barnum died in 1910, his circus continued to promote prodigies throughout the world, emulated in America by scores of travelling carnivals and sideshows which relentlessly criss-crossed the continent, seeking out new recruits as they went until no stone was left unturned. Deformed children, kept under lock and key for years, were suddenly seen as valuable commodities and eagerly rented out or sold by their parents. In the sideshows they found a true home, living and working with their own kind, creating a dark parallel society whose attraction never failed to pull in the leering crowds, 'normal' folk unwittingly gazing into the mirror of their hidden selves.

Other top retinues in the first part of the century included the Ringling Bros. Circus, the Clyde Beatty Circus, Sells Floto Circus and Al G. Barnes' Circus, and famous sideshows were to be found at Dreamland, Coney Island, and in Robert L. Ripley's itinerant *Believe It Or Not!*. Freaks were imported from all over the world for these revues, and America sustained its appeal as the global mecca for Nature's outsiders.

Nate Eagle, an impresario who specialised in handling midgets and dwarfs, had a troupe of around 300 members, whom he housed in a travelling series of 'midget villages', where the houses and streets were all scaled down to size, culminating with an exhibition at the 1934 Chicago World's Fair. In Gibsonton, Florida, successive seasons of carnival folk using the town as

Sideshow barker with pinhead, 1938

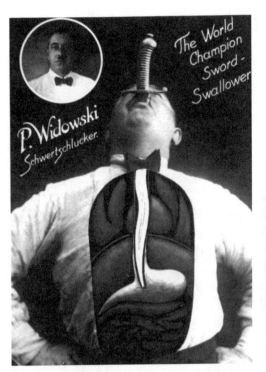

winter quarters led to it becoming a veritable haven for sideshow performers, and it earned the reputation of containing 'more freaks per square mile' than any other area in the world.

Meanwhile, as demand for human oddities grew, more and more 'self-made' freaks joined the ranks of those created by Nature. Koo-Koo, the "Bird Girl", and Betty Green, the "Stork Woman", who both appeared in Tod Browning's *Freaks*, were notable examples (acquiring a grotesque persona by costume, make-up and exaggeration); another was Mortado, the "Human Fountain", who actually had holes bored through his hands and feet so that water could pass through them, or he could be 'crucified'. Wooden plugs kept the holes from sealing. These acts, along with the likes of Pujol, the Parisian petomane, Widowski the Sword Swallower, or others who swallowed swords, or fish and lizards like Mac Norton, or drank petrol, or made their eyes stand out on stalks like "Popeye" Perez, were really not far removed from the lowest of the low in the unspoken hierarchy of carnival acts – the geek.

The geek was a generally down-and-out, commonly alcoholic or simple-minded man (or woman) whose act consisted of them sitting in a stinking bone-pit, dressed like deranged nightmare children, where they

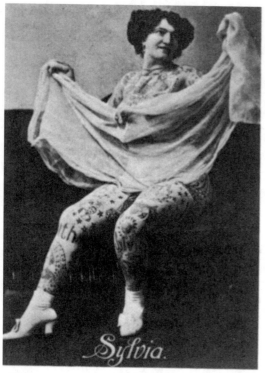

Sylvia

Surita

would draw a crowd of horrified/fascinated onlookers by biting the heads off live rats, chickens, or even snakes. While some geeks were so wasted they needed to be fed by hand, others prided themselves on catching and tearing apart their prey with their bare hands (these were known as "glommin' geeks"). Top geeks, not content with the kill, would then eat the animal raw, crunching the bones between their teeth and smearing their faces with hot blood and viscera, or vomiting back undigested fur, feathers and gristle. One such geek was the infamous Bosco, who reportedly ate live snakes. More recently, one Veronica Shant achieved wide renown for her feral appetites; she was reportedly a virginal, church-going saint outside the pit. Geeking, unsurprisingly, was among the first carnival acts to be outlawed as the 20th century unfurled.

The largest group of self-made freaks remains the tattooed men and ladies, those who have had themselves 'illustrated' from head to foot to create a new, almost living, skin. As early as 1890, the American Irene Woodward (1863-1916) was touring as "The Beautiful Irene". Other tattooed ladies

Maud Arizona

included Sylvia, Surita, Emma de Burgh, Englishwoman Anny Frank, the German Marie Theissen ("The Pearl of the Rhein"), Maud Arizona, Alwanda, Wallona Aritta, Creola, Angelika, Celly d'Astra, Arabella, and Anetta Nerona. Then there were tattooed men such as Don Manuelo, Rasmus Nielson, and Richardo, the "Living Tapestry".

None of these, however, could surpass the achievement of Sir Horace Rider, the Englishman who, in 1922, submitted his entire body to the needle of the famous London tattooist George Burchett and emerged, 150 hours and 100 plastic surgery operations later, as The Great Omi. A former army officer, the man had apparently inherited and then squandered a fortune after World War I. Unable to re-enter the army, he drew one last inspiration from carnival life, his abiding interest, and had himself tattooed in a unique and extraordinary way – having every inch of his skin, including eye cavities, throat and genitals, etched with dark, one-inch wide zebra-like stripes and swirls. The Great Omi travelled the world with a succession of shows and circuses, becoming one of the highest-paid acts ever to appear and also exhibiting himself for war charities and other causes.

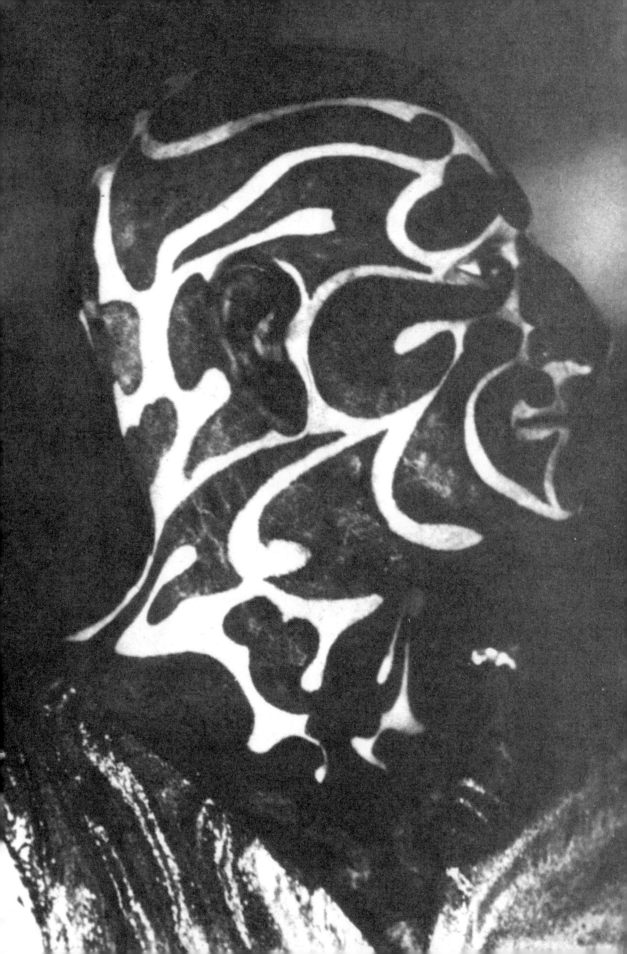

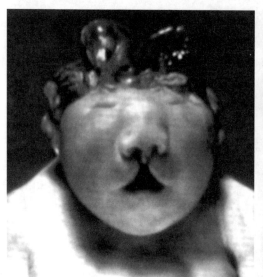 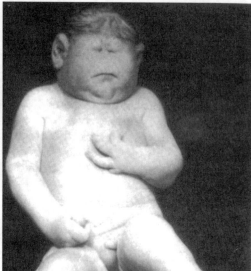

Two "pickled punks"

NOTES

1. Joseph Boruwlaski (1739–1837), the Tom Thumb of his day, travelled extensively through Europe and the Turkish Empire. Talks and concerts were apparently the source of his livelihood. He was a talented dancer and master of the violin. He stood 39 inches tall in adulthood and was said to have been eight inches long at birth. He lived into his 98th year.

2. Deformed foetuses, usually preserved in formaldehyde – "pickled punks" in carnival terminology – have always been a mainstay of both teratological research and sideshows alike. Many foetuses show deformities far beyond those displayed by the living – deformities simply too severe to allow the unborn child to survive.

3. This mystical reverence towards the malformed typifies the shamanistic qualities consistently attributed to them throughout the ages. Actual shamans in various cultures have indeed used physical difference to accentuate their oracular status, hermaphrodism being particularly desirable. This is achieved through complete castration, or sometimes by slitting and inverting the penis to resemble an exposed vulva. Western culture typically twisted this, establishing the stereotypical ugly, hump-backed appearance of the witch as proof of malevolence. Even so, atavistic traces of this relationship reside in our fascination with freaks, a deep-seated notion that their difference somehow exposes them to arcane knowledge or power.

TWO:
TAXONOMY

Classification of Human Anomalies • Golden Age of the
Freakshow

When science eventually overtook superstition in the categorisation and diagnosis of prodigies and marvels, the old myths were discarded and the remaining 'monsters' finally became 'human anomalies'. Among the main types of anomaly and condition identified in this new teratology were:

Hypertrichosis (and sundry zoomorphism):

Those suffering from this condition are the 'dog-men' and 'ape-women'; unfortunates born with an acute, bestial surplus of hair on their faces and bodies. Famous examples have included Horace Gonzales, an Italian living in Rome in the early 17th century, whose features were recorded for posterity in a celebrated engraving by the Florentine engraver Stephano Della Bella (1610-64). One of the earliest and most exact known representations of hypertrichosis, it ensured Gonzales' place in the annals of teratology. Another immortalised effigy is that of Tognina d'Ambras, the 'lion-faced girl', from the legendary family of hypertrichotics, by courtesy of the artist Giacomo Franco (c1580).

Portrait of Tognina d'Ambras

Jo-Jo, the dog-faced boy

Among their famous successors were Jo-Jo (1870-1903), the 'dog-faced boy', also known as the 'Poodle-Man' during his stint with Barnum; Lionel (1890-1932), the 'lion-man', real name Stéphane Bibrowski; Adrian Jerticheff, the 'dog of the Caucasus', who was first exhibited in Paris around 1873, sired an identical son (Jo-Jo), and believed himself the victim of a satanic curse; and the Malphoons, a whole family of Burmese 'dog-men' spanning three generations, who were exhibited in Paris throughout 1889.

Perhaps the strangest (and saddest) case of all was that of Julia Pastrana, the 'Gorilla-woman'. Alternatively known as the 'dog woman' or the 'ugliest woman in the world', Pastrana was born in Mexico in 1832 and, despite her looks, was by all accounts very sensitive and intelligent. She was discovered by an impresario, Theodore Lent, who became her manager and inducted her into show business. She soon became famous – and extremely profitable – and in order to keep his prize exhibit, Lent finally decided to marry her. Julia became pregnant, and eventually gave birth to a hairy, grimacing monster baby. Both mother and infant died in child-birth, and her last words are quoted as being: "I die happy, for I know I have been loved for

Lionel, the lion-man

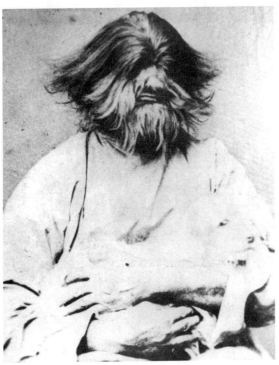

Adrian Jertichoff, the dog of the Caucasus

myself alone." Yet the tragic tale does not end there. Lent, determined to get his money's worth, had the two corpses embalmed, attired them in extravagant finery and toured them around Europe in a double crystal glass coffin. When the badly-preserved corpses started to rot, Lent had them stuffed and mummified like hunting trophies; after several more years touring these grisly remains, he eventually sold them off. The bodies now belong to an American collector. Lent also found a living replacement

The Malphoons

Julia Pastrana

Zenora Pastrana

for Julia; discovering Marie Bartels, a similarly hairy woman from Karlsbad, he re-christened her Zenora Pastrana and whisked her away to be his latest money-spinning exhibit. Lent died in 1884. [The extraordinary story of Julia Pastrana was filmed nearly a century later as *La Donna Scimmia*]

In Pastrana's footsteps came another female oddity: Krao, the 'chimpanzee-girl'. Born in Laos in 1872, she was discovered by one Karl Bock, and a description of her in *Nature* magazine, May 12 1883, reads:

"Her whole body is covered with smooth, straight black hair; her jaw is very prominent; her ability to push the lips out is developed to almost the same extent as a chimpanzee, and the set of her mouth, when she is annoyed, is quite characteristic; lastly, she has a prehensile foot, which she uses to pick the smallest objects off the ground."

Krao went on to star in Barnum and Bailey's circus before dying in New York, in 1926. Other hairy women, or 'bearded ladies', have included Helena Anthonia (c1600), Margareta von Parma, Magdeleine Ventura (painted by Ribera in 1631), Josephine Clofullia, Madame Clémentine Delait

Karl Bock and Krao

Anna Kritch, the bearded dwarf   *Unknown bearded Russian lady*

(1865-1939), Anna Kritch (the bearded dwarf), Juliane Sleebus, Madame Adriana, Milly Muro, Annie Jones (1865-1902, a Barnum exhibit), peroxide-whiskered Grace Gilbert (1880-1925) and Olga Roderick (who appeared in the film *Freaks*). Most recent of all was Puerto Rican Percilla Santher, who formed the bearded half of a bizarre marriage when she wed Emmett Bejano, the 'alligator-man' from Barnum in the '40s. She appears in Robert Kaylor's film *Carny* (1980).

Similar in appeal to the hypertrichotics, and usually billed as 'wild people', were the albinos, those with white hair, white skin and red eyes – sometimes referred to as the "night people" or "ice people". In America, Ada Russel (1873-1921) was an albino of great renown, as was Rob Roy (born 1866), who toured Europe with Barnum and Bailey in 1898, and Rolla, the 'albino princess'. Best known of them all was Tom Jack The Ice King, born Karl Breu *c.*1876. Tom Jack toured the world with Barnum and Bailey, was

Emmet Bejano and Percilla Santher   *Percilla's pin-up*

at one time assistant to Houdini, and later changed his name again to Toya, touring with his albino "Ice Family". Others of note included: Eliane Turnery, Princess Mitty, the Norwegian Mella Knudsen, Maud Mills (born 1899, Wyoming), Liliane (born in 1907, married the giant Peter Tom in 1929), albino twins Thelma and Doris, and last but not least the brothers Eko and Iko, a pair of negroid albinos from Ecuador who were regularly billed as the "sheep-headed cannibals". Albino negroes were also exhibited for their patchy pigmentation, and given such appellations as the "Leopard-boy" and the "Tiger-women".

Other 'jungle people' were rather less convincing; Waino and Plutano, the so-called "Wild Men of Borneo", were in reality a pair of hirsute midget grapplers from Long Island. True feral children, those raised in the wild by animals, have seldom been authenticated; alleged examples have included Amala and Kamala (the "Wolf-girls of Midnapore"), Lucas (the Baboon boy), and various "gazelle boys".[1]

Tom Jack the Ice King

Eko and Iko

Three Tiger Ladies

Another group often presented as wild people (although they are almost invariably child-like and harmless) are microcephalics: in other words, Pinheads (sometimes called "bird-heads"). The only group of show freaks who are congenitally mentally retarded, they have 'owners' as opposed to 'managers' and are usually asexual, the males and females often attired alike in dresses, hair shaved to a beribboned top-knot (a trend instigated by P. T. Barnum). They can behave erratically, and are sometimes kept chained to their keepers for their own safety. The most historically famous pinhead was named Triboulet, court jester to Francis I of France in the 1500s. He is said to have resembled a monkey, and his tall pointed hat is the model for the traditional 'dunce's cap'. Show pinheads have included: Bartola and Maximo, the Aztec Children; Godino and Apexia; Hattie and Tain; Assra, the amazing dwarf pinhead; Zip, Barnum and Bailey's "missing link" (a negro pinhead, habitually attired in a furry jumpsuit), teamed with Pip for *Freaks*, which also featured the Snow Twins Jennie and Elvira, and the famous "transvestite pinhead" Schlitzie. Schlitzie (mental age: 3) dressed as a woman in skirts so his nappies could be changed more easily. He also appeared in the film *Meet Boston Blackie* (1941).

Schlitzie on the set of "Meet Boston Blackie"

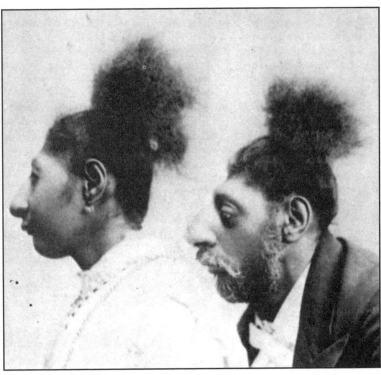

Assra, the dwarf pinhead

Bartola and Maximo

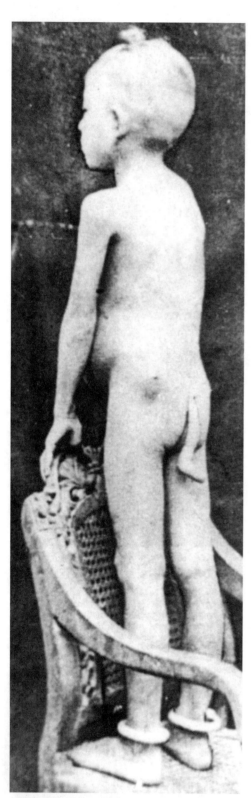

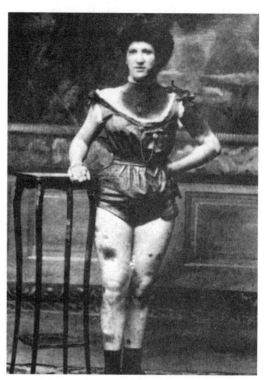

Irma Lousteau, the panther-woman

Liou Tang, the pig-boy   *Hoppie, the frog-boy*

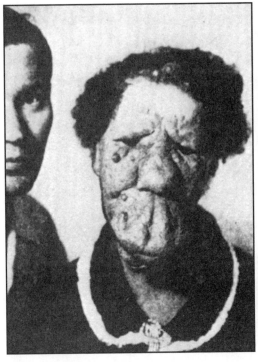 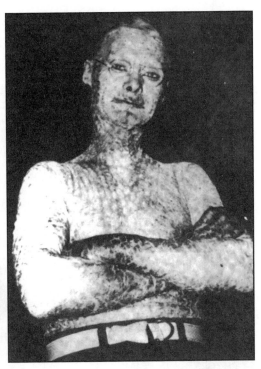

Grace McDaniel, the mule-headed woman   *John H Williams, the alligator-man*

Aside from the dog-boys, monkey-girls, bird-people and others, a whole range of different zoomorphs have cropped up in the carnival pantheon, most notably: "pig-boys" with snouts, tusks or curly tails (such as Liou Tang, the eight-tear-old Chinese boy with a foot-long tail); "spider-boys", scurrying crab-like across the midway; the legendary "biped armadillo"; Irma Lousteau, the "panther-woman" marked with random outcrops of fur; Hoppie, the "Frog-boy"; Grace McDaniel, the "mule-headed" woman, so named for her spectacular facial deformity (attributed to a "birthmark" with some understatement); Miss Violet (born 1888) and Lucy Elvira Jones, the double-jointed "Camel-girls", and their male counterpart Pony Boy; Miss Mignon, the "Penguin-lady"; Serpentina, the "snake-girl" with no bones other than in her head and neck; ectrodactylac Grady Stiles, the "Lobster Boy", proud to descend from five generations of Lobster People;[2] Mrs. Banks, the "bear-cub"; Sealo, the "Seal Boy", named for his flipper-like arms; "alligator-men" such as Emmett Bejano and John H Williams, who suffer from a condition known as *ichthyosis*; and "elephant-skinned" people such as the Englishman John

Miss Violet and Lucy Elvira Jones, the camel-girls

Pony Boy

Merrick ("The Elephant Man"), Anna C. Schmidt and Miss Susie (born Vienna, 1904). Legend even tells of a "shark-boy", a repugnant fish-skinned hermaphrodite deemed too hideous to even be exhibited.

Serpentina, the snake-girl

Mrs Banks, the bear-cub

Other skin conditions have included "elastic skin", as exhibited by Peter Spanner (born 1875), James Morris (part of Barnum's 1882 revue), Harry Haag, Etta Lake and Arthur Loose (one of the stars of Ripley's "Believe It Or Not!" show at the Chicago World's Trade Fair, 1933), and have also accounted for grotesque 'one-offs' such as the "Knotty Man" and others. Humans born *without* skin have seldom survived more than a few days at most, and only survive as "pickled punks" in medical facilities.

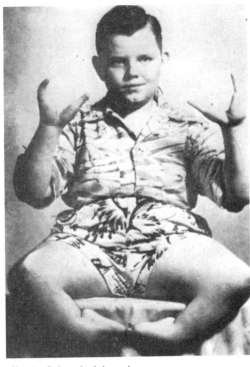

Grady Stiles, the lobster boy

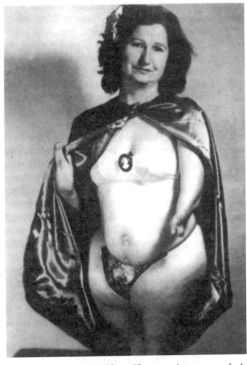

Miss Mignon, the penguin lady

Miss Susie and Agnes Schmidt, the girls with the elephant skin

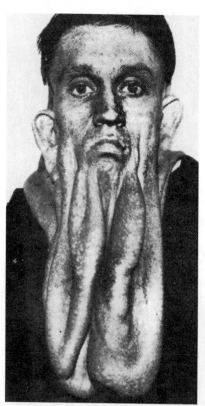 

Arthur Loose (left), Harry Haag (top right), Peter Spanner and Etta Lake

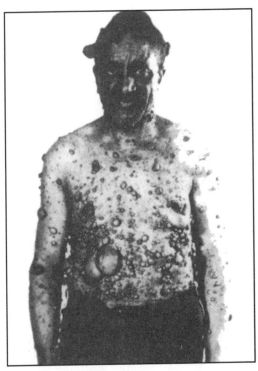
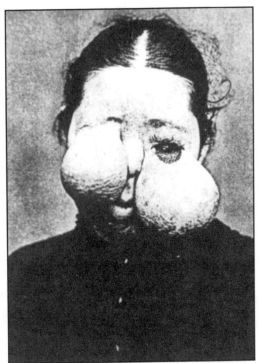

The Knotty Man   *Unidentified*

John Merrick (born Joseph Carey in 1862), whose story was famously filmed by David Lynch (*The Elephant Man*, 1980) remains England's most famous human anomaly. His "elephant skin" was due to an advanced condition of congenital Proteus syndrome and possibly additional neuro-fibromatosis. In his true account published in 1923, surgeon Sir Frederick Treves described the unfortunate young man as follows:

"He had a fleshy appendage hanging down from his forehead like an elephant's trunk. A spongy growth covered his neck. He was completely hairless. His forehead covered one eye. A mass of bone from the roof of his mouth projected out from his upper jaw. He had no nose. His body was hung with sacks of wrinkled skin. His right hand resembled a fin. His feet were too swollen to allow him to walk except by a shuffling gait. In addition, he had been dropped when a baby and his backbone was twisted out of shape." [see Appendix One for full text]

Merrick's own short "autobiography" – which appeared on the back of a freakshow pamphlet – reads as follows:

"I first saw the light on the 5th of August, 1860, I was born in Lee Street, Wharf Street, Leicester. The deformity which I am now exhibiting was caused by my mother being frightened by an Elephant; my mother was going along the street when a procession of Animals were passing by, there was a terrible crush of people to see them, and unfortunately she was pushed under the Elephant's feet, which frightened her very much; this occurring during a time of pregnancy was the cause of my deformity.

The measurement around my head is 36 inches, there is a large substance of flesh at the back as large as a breakfast cup, the other part in a manner of speaking is like hills and valleys, all lumped together, while the face is such a sight that no one could describe it. The right hand is almost the size and shape of an Elephant's foreleg, measuring 12 inches round the wrist and 5 inches round one of the fingers; the other hand and arm is no larger than that of a girl ten years of age, although it is well proportioned. My feet and legs are covered with thick lumpy skin, also my body, like that of an Elephant, and almost the same colour, in fact, no one would believe until they saw it, that such a thing could exist. It was not perceived much at birth, but began to develop itself when at the age of 5 years.

I went to school like other children until I was about 11 or 12 years of age, when the greatest misfortune of my life occurred, namely – the death of my mother, peace to her, she was a good mother to me; after she died my father broke up his home and went to lodgings; unfortunately for me he married his landlady; henceforth I never had one moment's comfort, she having children of her own, and I not being so handsome as they, together with my deformity, she was the means of making my life a perfect misery; lame and deformed as I was, I ran, or rather walked away from home two or three times, but suppose father had some spark of parental feeling left, so he induced me to return home again. The best friend I had in those days was my father's brother, Mr. Merrick, hair Dresser, Church Gate, Leicester.

When about 13 years old, nothing would satisfy my step-mother until she got me out to work; I obtained employment at Messrs. Freeman's Cigar Manufacturers, and worked there about two years, but my right hand got too heavy for making cigars, so I had to leave them. I was sent about the town to see if I could procure work, but being lame and deformed no one would employ me; when I went home for my meals, my step-mother used to say I had not been to seek for work. I was taunted and sneered at so that I would not go home for

Two views of John Merrick, The Elephant Man

my meals, and used to stay in the streets with an hungry belly rather than return for anything to eat, what few half-meals I did have, I was taunted with the remark – "That's more than you have earned."

Being unable to get employment my father got me a pedlar's license to hawk the town, but being deformed, people would not come to the door to buy my wares. In consequence of my ill luck my life was again made a misery to me, so that I again ran away and went hawking on my own account, but my deformity had grown to such an extent, so that I could not move about the town without having a crowd of people gather around me. I then went into the infirmary at Leicester, where I remained for two or three years, when I had to undergo an operation on my face, having three or four ounces of flesh cut away; so thought I, I'll get my living by being exhibited about the country. Knowing Mr. Sam Torr, Gladstone Vaults, Wharf Street, Leicester, went in for Novelties, I wrote to him, he came to see me, and soon arranged matters, recommending me to Mr. Ellis, Bee-hive Inn, Nottingham, from whom I received the greatest kindness and attention.

In making my first appearance before the public, who have treated me well – in fact I may say I am as comfortable now as I was uncomfortable before. I must now bid my kind readers adieu."

John Merrick died in 1890, suffocating in his sleep under the sheer weight of his own skull.

Autository, or 'double' monsters:

In other words, Siamese twins. The term 'Siamese twins' actually originates from the famous xiphopages Chang and Eng, born in Siam in 1811 (their names simply mean 'left' and 'right' in Chinese), although the earliest authenticated case dates right back to 1100, a pair of sisters born in England by name of Helisa and Mary Chulkurst. The anatomist Luigi Galvani reputedly possessed a pickled, three-headed foetus, while it is reported that King James IV of Scotland greatly favoured a certain subject whose body was 'single below, with only two legs, but had two chests and two heads'. Sebastian Münster recorded an unusual case in his *Cosmographiae Universalis* (1544), but the first to be scrutinized scientifically appear to have been Hélène and Judith, born in 1701, who feature in Buffon's *Histoire Naturelle*. When they died in 1723, an autopsy revealed that they had but a single anus, and two vaginas which merged into a single vulva. Such physical anomalies have since been found to be common in Siamese Twins; one pair of baby girls separated in 1974 having no fewer than four vaginas between them. Common types of Siamese twins include craniopages (joined at the head), xiphopages (joined at the side or chest), gastropages (joined at the stomach) and pygopages (joined at the pelvis). Less common are ischiopages,

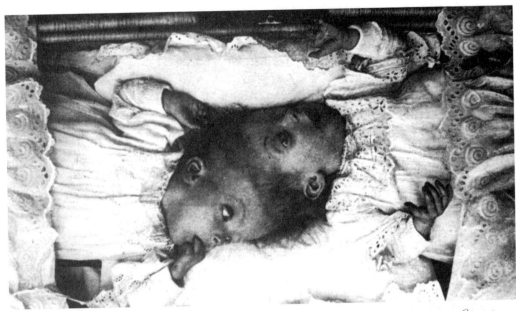

Craniopages

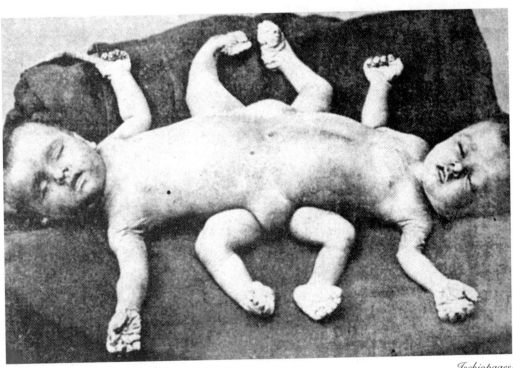

Ischiopages

bodies totally fused into one to give the impression of a two-headed, eight-limbed human spider, whose incredibly complex nature renders separation impossible. Always of the same sex, there have been unsubstantiated reports

Chang and Eng   *Liou Tang-Sen and Liou Seng-Sen*

of hermaphrodite Siamese twins, each combining male and female gender.

Other famous examples have included Elizabeth Bedbury, a two-headed lady born in 1842 in Surrey (exhibited at the notorious Bartholomew's Fair in Smithfield, London), the Indians Gangalai and Gourabai, the Russians Macha and Dacha, the Cubans Kenerado and Rivero, the gastropage brothers Liou-Tang-Sen and Liou-Seng-Sen (Barnum & Bailey exhibits), multi-talented English pygopages Violet and Daisy Hilton (who appear in Tod Browning's *Freaks*), pygopages Josepha-Rosa Blazek (performers at the *Théâtre de la Gaité* in 1890's Paris), the Mexican gastropages Mary and Arrita, black American sisters Millie and Christine (born in slavery and otherwise known as the "United African Twins"), and Lucio and Simplicio Godina. These last two were brothers born in 1906 in the Phillipines, and came to Europe in 1930. They married normal twin sisters, and danced the tango as a foursome, becoming champion ice-skaters. But one brother got drunk at the wheel, and knocked over a child. He escaped a prison sentence, since it was deemed unfair to also incarcerate the innocent twin,

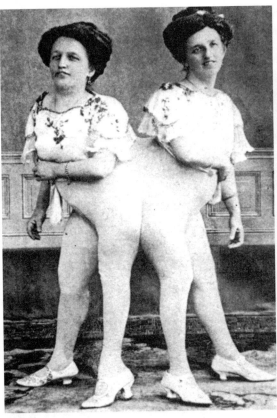

Josepha-Rosa Blazek

Millie and Christine

and a hefty fine was imposed instead. His brother then refused to perform any longer, to which the other responded with a suicide threat. In the end, Simplicio died first, in 1936. Lucio had the corpse surgically removed, but perished 11 days after. It is reported that Chang and Eng were dogged by similar problems, being forced to quit America to escape the attentions of one Miss Gloria, a raving nymphomaniac obsessed with the potential of their double genitalia. They eventually married two women who disliked each other, and had to visit them in turn, riding to their separate homes which each boasted a king-sized bed for three; they nonetheless sired a reputed twenty-two children between them.

Probably the most remarkable of 'double-monsters' was a derodym, the strange being known as Giovanni and Giacomo Tocci. Born October 4th 1877 in Sardinia, the Toccis consisted of two identical heads atop a splayed, V-shaped torso fitted with four arms, supported by a single pelvis and two

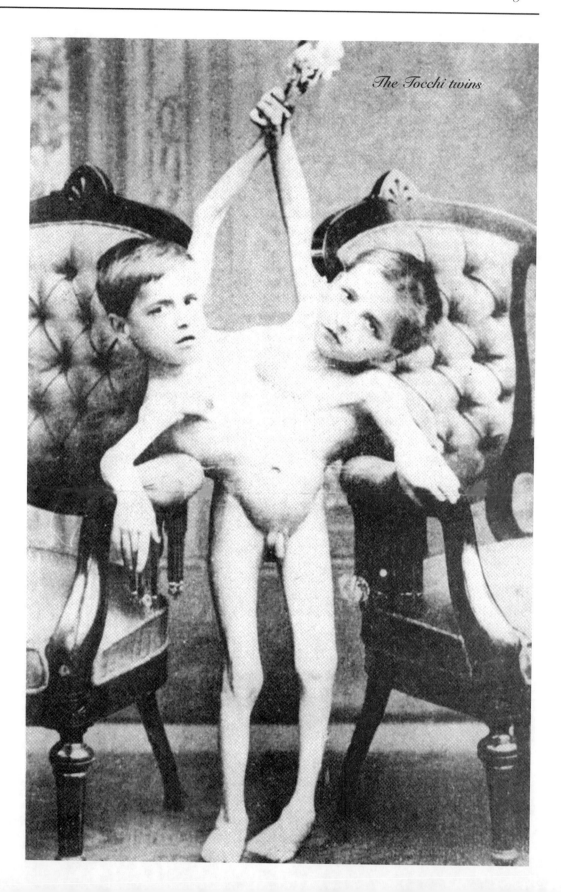

The Tocchi twins

legs. They also sported a third buttock, and were generally incapable of perambulation due to atrophy. Each head was duly baptised; Giovanni, on the right, was lively and intelligent, while Giacomo, to the left, was more slow-witted. In 1892, aged 15, they went to America, where the Scientific Academy pronounced them "the most remarkable double-monster to have ever reached maturity". In 1897 the Toccis returned to Italy and built themselves a high-walled house near Venice, and lived there having married two sisters (since they had two heads but only one penis, it would seem that each enjoyed the other's bride). They lived until 1940, and died age 63.

Another example was Rita-Christina, born in 1829 in Sardinia; but this double creature, with two heads and bodies joined to a single lower half (a condition known as *dicephalus*), only lived to eight months.

In Maine, USA in 1940, doctors recorded the live birth of twins whose faces were completely fused; they survived for only a few hours.

More recent cases of united twins have included Mary and Margaret Gibb, Lotti and Rosemarie Knaack, Donald and Ronald Gaylon, Santina and Giuseppina Foglia, Clara and Alta Rodriguez[3], and black American craniopages Yvonne and Yvette, born in Los Angeles in 1949, whose parents held a party in 1961 to celebrate the first million dollars earned from exhibiting their offspring.

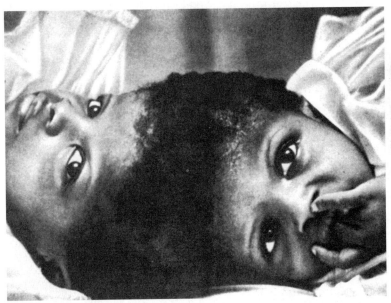

Yvonne and Yvette

Face-fused twin

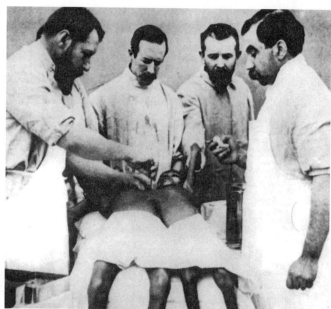

Radica and Doodica   *Dr. Doyen operates*

Separating Siamese twins surgically has always been a pre-occupation amongst doctors and surgeons. The main problem is that twins of this nature often have only one heart, one liver, one set of intestines etc, so that there are insufficient organs to support two separate entities. The first recorded attempt dates from 1701, when a certain Dr. Treyling operated on two sisters, Magdelena and Suzanna, joined at the base of the spine. They died. Most notorious of all was the attempt made in Paris in 1892 by Dr. Doyen to separate the famous Indian xiphopages Radica and Doodica Orissa. Born in 1888, these sisters had been hounded from their native home by the locals, who believed their affliction to be a divine curse. Priests gave them sanctuary, believing them to be demi-goddesses, but eventually sold them to a London impresario who exhibited them in the Tuileries in 1892. When Doodica succumbed to tuberculosis, Dr. Doyen of the Trousseau hospital announced that he would operate to part them. The operation become a public spectacle, a grand event with Doyen – quickly dubbed the "Barnum of surgery" by his rivals – performing before the cameras in what could perhaps be regarded as the first genuine exploitational photography of human anomalies. The operation was not a success; Doodica succumbed under the knife, and Radica was dead within two years. The first successful separation was achieved in 1952; it is now a commonplace and generally safe practice.

Lazarus-Johannes Batista Colleredo

A most extraordinary type of Siamese twins are 'parasitic monsters'. These fall into two main categories: heteradelphians and pygomelians. Both are born with half-formed siblings extruding from their own bodies. Early recorded examples of the former were Hans Kaltenbrunn, born in 1525 with a parasitic brother hanging from his belly, and Lazarus-Johannes Batista Colleredo, born in Genoa in 1617. Colleredo's parasite, unusually, had a head. Michel Montaigne, who witnessed one of these creatures first-hand, left the following account amongst his essays:

Laloo   *Perumal*   *Jacques Liberra*

"*This tale shall speak for itself, for I shall leave its discussions to the physicians. Two days ago I saw a child being led about by two men and a nurse, who said they were his father, his uncle, and his aunt, in order to make a few pence by displaying him, because of his strangeness. In all else, he conducted himself normally, he stood on his feet, walked, and chattered more or less like all children of his age: he had never taken nourishment, except at his nurse's breast; and what was put in his mouth in my presence, he chewed a little, and put out again: his cries did indeed seem rather peculiar: he was exactly fourteen months old. Under his nipples he was fastened and joined to another child, which had no head, and had the conduit of its back stopped, the rest being whole; one of his arms was indeed shorter than the other, but it had been broken accidentally at birth: they were joined face to face, as if a younger child were trying to embrace another, older, one. The joint and space where they were joined was but four inches across, or thereabouts, so that if you lifted the imperfect child up, you could see under the other's navel: so the joint was between his nipples and his navel. The navel of the imperfect one could not be seen, but all the rest of his belly could. So what was not joined, such as the arms, buttocks, thighs and legs of the imperfect one, hung free and swinging*

 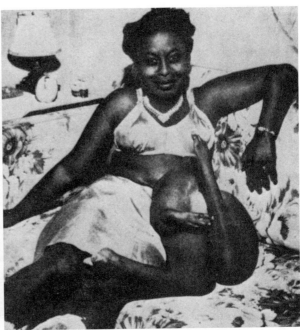

Betty Lou Williams

against the other, and could reach half-way down his leg. The nurse told us that he made water in both places, so the other one's limbs were nourished and living, and in the same state as his own, except that they were smaller and thinner."

One of first show-heteradelphians was the Indian boy Laloo (1869-1902), who came to London in 1882 to exhibit his headless twin. Though billed as a female, the twin was actually male and capable of urination and of sustaining an erection. Laloo perished in a Mexican train crash, in 1905. Another Indian was Perumal, who modestly exhibited in Europe with his headless parasite (named Sami) dressed in silks. Jean Liberra, born in Rome in 1884, became famous with Barnum & Bailey. His parasitic twin, Jacques, was very well developed, and whilst Liberra was in Berlin, a certain Professeur Berdenheimer X-rayed him. His conclusion was that the twin had a head-cage inside its host, and that technically it was alive. Liberra married, had four normal children, and died in 1946. Betty Lou Williams, a black American, was born in Atlanta with the remains of her twin sister protruding from her side. As she grew up, the twin (unusually) grew in proportion. By 1950, Betty Lou was earning $5,000 a month as an exhibit. She died in 1958, reputedly of a broken heart.

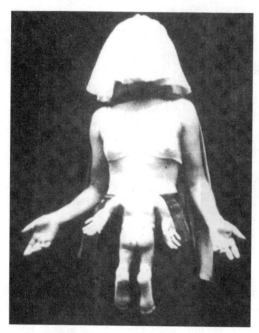

Margarete Clark, heteradelphian

Elsie Linn, pygomelian

Famous pygomelians – in whom only the legs or lower half of their twin is externalised – have included the American Myrtle Corbin, who boasted an extra pair of underdeveloped legs and two vaginas; Elsie Linn, who sported a third, deformed leg; the Cuban Jean Baptista dos Santos, born in 1845, who had extra sets of legs *and* fully-functional genitals; and, most renowned of all, Francesco A. Lentini, born in 1889 with an extra leg, virtually full-sized, sprouting from his right buttock. This leg also carried the atrophied remains of a vestigial fourth limb, giving him sixteen toes in all. He could control all three legs perfectly, and could ride a bicycle with ease. Lentini too was blessed with an extra (though reputedly underdeveloped) set of genitals. He came to America in 1898 and soon found fame and fortune, also marrying and siring four children. The creation of the three-legged stool was, reputedly, inspired by him. He died in Florida in 1964.

Other odd configurations have come to light. Exceptionally grotesque was the case of Edward Mordake, who is said to have been cursed with a "devil twin" – the shrunken head and face of a girl appended to the back of his head. The face was reputedly animated, and the thought of it drove him to an early suicide. The Mexican Pasqual Piñon was also apparently born with a small extra face, this one growing out of his forehead. Again, the eyes

The Great Lentini

moved and the mouth would open and close, though it withered in later life. A famous historical example is the so-called "Home's case", the double-skulled skeleton of an Indian infant.

Related to these individuals is the case of Bill Durks, an American born in 1930. Durks' extraordinary face shows the arrested beginnings of becoming two heads, or perhaps twins; he became a celebrated carnival attraction, and even took to painting a third eye in the gap between his divided nose. Durks died in 1976.

Finally, and most perhaps bizarre of all, comes the enigma of epignathic parasites, virtually formless pieces of human matter usually extruding from the host's mouth. They are a form of teratoma, very much like foetuses *in fetu*. These latter are thought to be tiny, macerated, barely-developed embryos lodged completely inside their living twins. In 1951, the case was reported of a male child found to be housing no less than five such vestigial siblings *within his cranium*. Two years later, Algerian doctors operating on a young boy for a 'stomach tumour' finally removed a six-inch-long male foetus; a number of similar cases have since been recorded.

Myrtle Corbin, pygomelian

The Hilton sisters, united twins

Chang and Eng with their wives and children

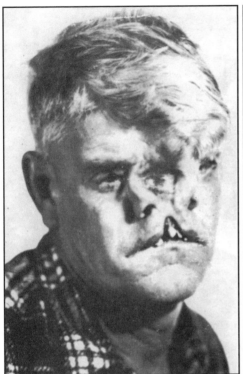

Bill Durks

Pascal Piñon

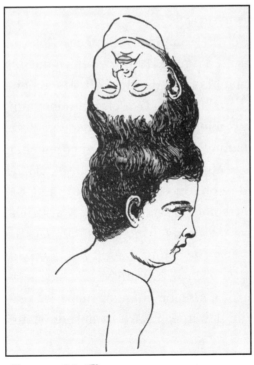

Drawing of the Homes case

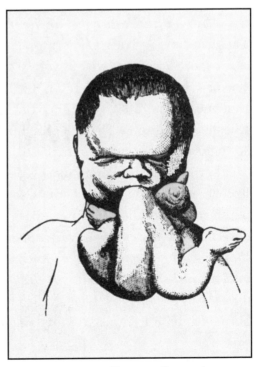

Drawing of epignathic monster

Charles Tripp and Eli Bowen

Symelians and Podurges, or 'half' monsters:

These are those born armless or legless, the completely limbless ("basket cases"), or those born with severely truncated limbs. Early examples include Thomas Schweiker (1541-1602), Catherina Mazzina (born 1577), Magdalena Emohne (born 1596), Matthias Buchinger (born 1674), Peter Stadelmann, Elisabeth Simson, Theodor Steib, Bartholomé, Philippe Ludovic Herr, Antonius Maria Reuter (born 1716), Johann Jacob Ewerth, the phocomelian ('seal-armed') Petit-Pépin (born Marco Catozze in 1741), scourge of the French court circa 1775, Louis César Joseph Ducornet (1806-56), and the peromelian Rosalie Fournier, born November 12th 1813 in Marseilles, described in her show advertisement as *"a living female without legs or thighs, with a woman's breast and nipple on the end of the left-hand stump, and a coral-shaped ear-ring of flesh on the right"*. In reality, her feet grew directly from her hips. Legend also tells of a sirenomelian, or mer-creature, born with both legs fused into a single limb, but there are no authenticated cases.

Ann Leak Thomson

John Chambert

Armless notables include Ann Leak Thomson, saxophonist James Elroy, John Chambert (born 1854), Anton Pohl, Annie Lee, the Russian Rebecca Stromynka, Margarete Mariot, Luis Steinkogler, Gazay the Great, the Japanese Oguri Kiba, Tommy "Toes" Jacobsen, Frances O'Connor (born 1917, a regular with the Cole Brothers circus) and Martha Morris, who both appeared in *Freaks*, Canadian Charles Tripp (1855-1939), Freddie Esele ("The Armless Wonder"), and perhaps the greatest of them all, Carl Hermann Unthan. Born in 1848, Unthan became known as the 'armless violinist of Leipzig', and was also accomplished in many other activities. He went on to appear in the Danish film version of Gerhardt Hauptmann's novel *Atlantis* (August Blom, 1913), and in the German film *Der Mann Ohne Arme* (also 1913). His autobiography, *Das Pediskript*, was published in 1925. He died in 1929, in Berlin. Best-known of the show phocomelians were Andy, the "Sea-Lion", and Sealo, the "Seal Boy", a Ringling Bros. regular.

Tod Browning's *Freaks* brought notoriety to one Prince Randian, the Living Torso, born without limbs, but who nonetheless sired five children by his devoted wife. Though he could only move by wriggling along the ground like a worm, Randian could perform various tricks with his mouth including

Gazay The Great

Frances O'Connor

Freddie Esele

Carl Hermann Unthan

Andy, the Sea-Lion   *Sealo, the Seal-Boy*   *James Elroy*

rolling and lighting a cigarette. He died in 1934, aged 63, after appearing at Sam Wagner's 14th Street Museum.

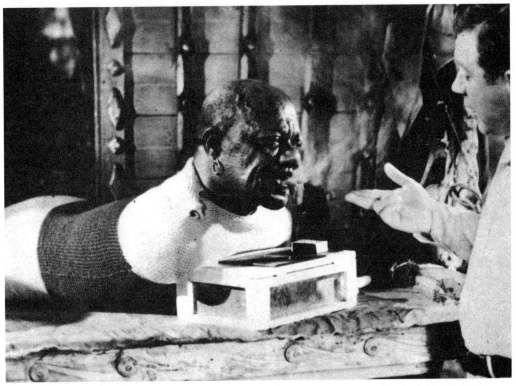

Randian, the Living Torso, in the film "Freaks"

Kobelkoff

Thomas Goy

Miss Marta

Frieda Puschnik

Violetta

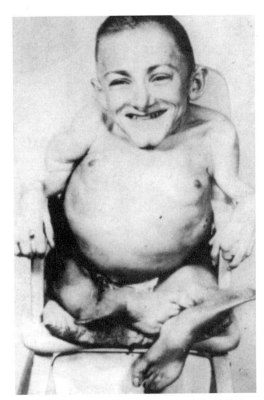

Jonn Doogs aka Nicodemus

Lloyd Skelton

One of the other most famous 'human trunks' was Kobelkoff, born in Siberia in 1851 with only a right shoulder-stump to speak of. Yet his show repertoire included tapestry-weaving, painting and rifle-shooting. He married one Anna Wilfert in 1876, giving her fifteen children and allegedly beating her with his stump when angry. He died in 1933. Other 'living torsos' have included the Englishman Thomas Goy, the American Emmett, the Frenchman Pierre Mahieux, and such women as Marie Bury, Marta, Annitta, Frieda Puschnik, and the celebrated Violetta.

Others born with little or nothing below the waist have included John Doogs (aka Nicodemus, born 1869), Princess Ida (born 1879), Sandu, Jeanie the half-girl (who married the giant, Al Tomaini in 1936), Tiny LaVonda, Lloyd Skelton, Lilli the Living Bust, and Eli Bowen (born 1844), who famously teamed up with the armless Charles Tripp to ride a special bicycle, with Tripp pedalling while Eli steered. Bowen, whose feet grew direct from his hips, was also an accomplished acrobat.

Sandu

Lilli, the Living Bust   *Eli Bowen*

Perhaps the most famous half-boy of all time is Johnny Eck, another star of Tod Browning's *Freaks*; his remarkable and illuminating story is one of the most famous in carnival legend. Of all the human anomalies who appear in *Freaks*, none have caught the public's imagination so much as Eck, the 'most remarkable man alive', the self-styled 'King of the Freaks'. His life story, which begins one stormy August night in 1911, in Baltimore, is one of the most remarkable ever told and provides a telling complement to Browning's own black fable.

That summer night, a perfectly normal woman gave birth to twins; the first-born, Robert Eckhardt, weighed 6 pounds and was in fine health. Twenty minutes later the second child, who would be christened John, emerged, and by the scant illumination of chain lightning the nurse and other attendants could see that he was somehow much smaller than his twin brother; in fact, Johnny Eckhardt had been born weighing just 2 pounds, a "broken doll" with virtually no body whatsoever beneath the bottom of his rib-cage. Miraculously, he survived.

Johnny's family, though they were poor, did not desert their half-formed child; he was perfectly intelligent, and he and Robert were brought up and educated with care. Johnny learnt to walk on his hands, and was extremely athletic. From a young age, he liked to entertain, and was naturally drawn towards the travelling carnivals which came to town. He later recalled: *"When I saw those tents, that was the end of sitting at a desk for me. God, how I loved to get out under those big tents. I loved the animals and I loved camping out. Rob and me, we'd go over to the horse barn and get the sweetest-smelling hay for a bed, and we'd sit up late and shoot the breeze with some of the most wonderful people in the world. I met hundreds and thousands of people, and none finer than the midgets and the Siamese twins and the caterpillar man and the bearded woman and the human seal with the little flippers for hands. I never asked them any embarrassing questions and they never asked me, and God, it was a great adventure."*

One of the biggest days of Johnny's young life came in December 1923, when he and Robert were taken to see a big magic show in the local church. The act came to a premature close when Johnny jumped up on stage to claim a prize; the audience went wild, and the magician was so dumb-struck he was lost for words. Finally, he summoned Johnny's mother and offered to make her rich by letting him put her half-boy on the stage. This was to be Johnny's

John and Robert Eckhardt   *The Great Johnny Eck*

first bitter lesson of the cruelties and trickery of the carnival world he loved so dearly.

The magician had soon persuaded his mother to sign a contract making him Johnny's manager for 1 year; a figure which was later blatantly altered to read "10 years". Johnny's last name was shortened to Eck, for the stage; it was not the only thing to be reduced. The high salary promised turned out to be $20 a week, while the manager was raking in over $100 per day through exhibiting the boy prodigy. Johnny refused to continue after the first 12 months and, despite threats of legal action, escaped the magician's clutches – for a while. Aged 14, Johnny and Robert went off to work with Captain Sheesley's circus in Plainfield NJ, a far happier experience. Johnny, who had been painting and making wooden models since the age of 8, had by now added juggling, tightrope-walking, conjuring, acrobatics, animal-

Prince Randian and Johnny Eck on the set of "Freaks"

training and sax-playing to his incredible repertoire.

Then came the Great Depression. With Bob and Johnny out of work and back in Baltimore, the Eckhardt family were down on their luck and in danger of losing their home. Out of the blue, a letter from Johnny's ex-manager arrived, inviting him to pay a visit to Maryland. There was nothing to lose, and so Johnny accepted. He had a great time, and it seemed like the manager was a reformed man; not long after he came through with a booking, and Bob and Johnny found themselves bound for Canada, to appear at the National Exposition. It so happened that two talent scouts from MGM were at the shows, and they got Johnny to take a screen test. Within 4 weeks, the Eckhardt brothers were bound for California, where the shooting for Tod Browning's *Freaks* was about to commence.

Johnny recalled how right from the start he became Browning's favourite; the director would address him as "Mr. Johnny", and have him sit next to him at all times. Indeed, the whole crew loved the half-boy, and it was to be one of the happiest times of his life. He was the star of the show, without doubt, and even had his own private dressing room, emblazoned with 'The Great Johnny Eck'. Inevitably, it was all too good to be true; it turned out that Johnny's manager, who had negotiated the MGM deal, had secured himself *over 90%* of the star's salary – and Johnny estimated that he was being paid around $1,000 a week. Once again he had fallen prey to the type of merciless exploitation which was, sadly, all too commonplace in the world of carnivals and sideshows.

After shooting, Johnny returned to Baltimore. He soon heard that Browning was planning another film, in which he wanted the half-boy to star. But again, MGM were negotiating with the crooked manager. Determined not be exploited again, Johnny wrote to both the studio and his manager, demanding a fee of $600 a week; as a result, the deal fell through, and although Johnny did suit up for MGM's *Tarzan The Ape Man* (as a bird-creature), his Hollywood career was effectively at an end.

Johnny continued to work in the carnivals and road shows, performing with Robert L. Ripley of *Believe It Or Not* fame in Chicago, Cleveland and Dallas, and also touring with various magic acts (he was made to be 'sawn in half'). His other exploits included conducting an orchestra in his home town, and driving a midget racing car in fairs throughout the south. But Johnny increasingly believed that this way of life was endangered, that his innocent form of entertainment was out of step with public taste. He retired in 1940, later reflecting that "people wanted sex from then on... now it's crime, dope and filth," poignantly adding: "If I want to see freaks, all I have to do is look out the window."

As if to confirm his worst fears, Johnny was assaulted during a burglary on his Baltimore home in 1988, and subsequently became withdrawn and reclusive. He died three years later.

During his career he had made thousands of friends, both carnival workers and public alike; people who saw Johnny Eck not as a freak, but as a great performer, a friendly and genuine person, and a truly unique human being.

Tom Thumb and Lavinia Warren   *Prince Nicholi*

Dwarfs and Giants:

These are the most commonplace of human prodigies, with dwarfs in particular occurring in great number throughout the world even to this day. The most common kind are achondroplasic dwarfs, victims of a deforming, bone-truncating condition, while the name 'midget' is more usually given to those diminutive beings whose frames are in more harmonious proportion, resembling normal people in miniature. Other dwarfing conditions include spinal osteomyelitis (causing 'rachitics'), thyroid or ovarian deficiency, and metaphysical dysostosis. Dwarfs and midgets of renown have included: John Decker, Jimmy Camber (also notoriously fat), Hannah Warton, Jeffrey Hudson, Owen Farrel, Robert and Judith Skinner (1698-1763), John Coan (1728-64), Joseph Boruwlaski (1739-1837), Richebourg, Wybrand Lolkes, Hokins Hopkins (1736-54), Thomas Carter, Kelham Whitelamb, George Romondo, Nicolas Ferry, Catherina Helena Stoberin, Ignatz Ackenheil, Emma Leach, Calvin Philips, Nannette Stocker, Simon Paap (1789-1828), Tom Thumb (1838-83) and his wife Lavinia Warren, Thumb's love rival Commodore Nutt, Admiral Dot, Prince Nicholi (reputedly the smallest man

Lucia Zarate

Mr and Mrs Mite

ever, at 18" tall), Lucia Zarate (1864-1890, reputedly the smallest woman who ever lived), Count Magri, Major James Doyle, Carrie Akers (also obese), Mr. & Mrs. Mite, Smaun Sing Hpoo, Princess Pauline Masters (1876-95), Princess Elisabeth, Prince Puck, Princess Martha, the Speck Brothers, Franz

Smaun Sing Hpoo

Princess Martha

Prince Puck

Baron Magri; Count Magri; Lavinia Warren; Major James Doyle (seated)

and Carl Rossow, Princess Reta, Abdurrhama Pascha, Georg Theodor Ulpts, Prince Colibri (aka Dimitri Ossopoff), Millie Edwards, General Peanuts, Prince Mignon, Tiny Tim (aka Harold Pyott), Tom Sodrie, Fred "Pip" Aslett, Lia Graf (gassed by the Nazis), Walter Böning, Friedrich Hakl, Giuseppe Bignoli, Willy Rolle, Carl Norwood, Dolly Regan (the "ossified girl"), Caroline Cramachi, Charles Lockhart (three times Texas State Treasurer), Franz Ebert (who appeared on baby food labels), clowns Andrea Barnabé, Frankie

Princess Pauline   *Princess Reta*   *Kiki the clown*

The Speck Brothers   *Franz and Carl Rossow*

Saluto, Jimmy Armstrong, Pooh-Bah (aka Pete Terhune), Buddie Thompson, Ferry and Gin, and Kiki (aka Otto Moskowitz), and such troupes as the Liliput Revue, the Singer Midgets, the Doll Family, and John Lester's Midget Ladies.

The Doll Family: Daisy, Grace and Harry Earles

Portrait of Count Joseph Borulawski

*Portrait of Queen Henrietta Maria
and her pet dwarf, Jeffery Hudson*

*Portrait of the Irish dwarf
Owen Farrel*

*Portrait of Perkeo, the dwarf of
Heidelberg, with mandrill*

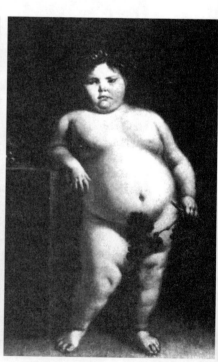

*Portrait of dwarf Eugenia Martinez
Vallejo as naked Bacchus*

Carrie Akers, the fat dwarf

Lia Graf

Waino and Plutano, the dwarf wrestlers

Dwarf jester (with Koo-Koo, the bird-girl)

Chang Yu-Sing   *Abomah*   *Robert Wadlow*

Giants, contrary to reputation, are seldom strong. Caused by pituitary deficiency, their condition very often renders them sluggish and clumsy. They are prone to acromegaly (a deforming skin condition) and kyphoscoliosis (crippling spinal curvature); poor circulation can often result in gangrene and limb amputation, and few specimens live to anything approaching old age. Giants and giantesses of renown have included: Anthony Payne, William Joyce, Anton Franck, Edmund Malone, Cornelius MacGrath (1736-52), Bernardo Gigli, Mrs. Gordon of Essex, Daniel Cajanus (a reputed, but unsubstantiated, 12' 1"), Charles Byrne, Edward Bamford, Basilio Huaylas from Peru, Thomas Bell, James Toller (1795-1819), Elizabeth Stock, Ann Hardy, Josef Behin, Louis Frenz, Joseph Brice (known as "Anak, King of the Anakims, Giant of Giants"), the Irishman James Murphy, Canadian sisters Amelia and Priscilla Weston, Martin Bates (1845-1919) and his partner Anna Swann (1846-88, who reputedly gave birth to Bates' still-born child 24 inches long and 27 pounds in weight), Chang Yu-Sing (1840-93), Ella Ewing, Carl Brustad, Joseph Drasal (1841-86), Louis Wilkins, Emanuel Andersson, Oswald Balling, Trante Victor, Abomah, Jakob Murdel (1874-1904), the

Van Albert

Eugene Berry

Russian Pisjakoff, Hugo, George Auger, Teddy Bobs, Waino Myllyrinne (1909-63), Angus McAskill, Dora Helms, Paul Herold, Jan Van Albert, Jack Earl, Henry Hite, Max Palmer, Robert Wadlow (an authenticated 8' 11"), Johann K. Petursson, Al Tomaini, Ted Evans, Eddie Carmel ("The Happy Giant"), Gabriel Munjane, and Dolores Pullard ("The Amazon Girl"). The American Eugene Berry (born 1872) was one of many stricken with elephantiasis, giving him giant and deformed appendages. The greatest authenticated height on record was achieved by the Russian Fédor Machnov (1881-1905), who measured in at an incredible 9' 4". His customary four meals a day consisted of two litres of tea, twenty eggs and eight buttered rolls for breakfast; two and a half kilos of meat, a kilo of potatoes and three litres of beer for lunch; a tureen of soup, another two and a half kilos of meat, three loaves of bread and two litres of tea for supper; and fifteen eggs with bread and a litre more of tea before bed.

Paul Herold
with Zip, the pinhead

Al Tomaini
with his wife, Jeannie the half-girl

George Auger
with the midget Tom Sodrie

Dolores Pullard, the Amazon girl

Machnov, the Russian giant

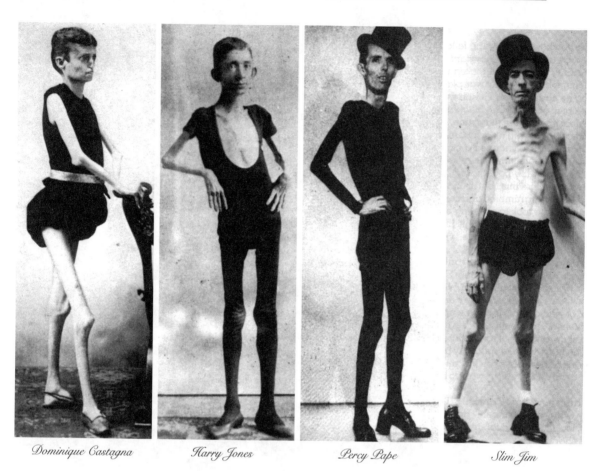

Dominique Castagna   Harry Jones   Percy Pape   Slim Jim

Sharing the polar physical relationship of midgets to giants are the extremely thin and extremely fat people who have come to prominence throughout history. Famous thin men have included: Claude-Ambroise Seurat, the "Living Skeleton", who lived in early 19th century France and was reputedly 3 inches thick; Calvin Edson; Isaac Spragues, born 1841, who weighed 44 pounds; Harry V. Lewis; James Coffey; John Darrington; the Austrian Carl Noisée, born 1861; Dominique Castagna, who weighed just 50 pounds but still managed to hang himself in 1907; Eddie Masher, the "Skeleton Dude", who weighed 38 pounds; Harry Jones, born 1860, who weighed 49 pounds; Percy Pape, born 1932, who weighed 68 pounds and by 1960 had sustained over 75 limb fractures; Milton "Slim Jim" Malone (68 pounds); Mac Intosh; Pete Robinson, weighing 64 pounds, who in 1933 married circus fat lady Bunny Smith (518 pounds); and Glen Pulley, weighing 72 pounds, who also married a fat lady weighing nearly 600 pounds. A rare example of a professional thin lady was Rosa Lee Plemons.

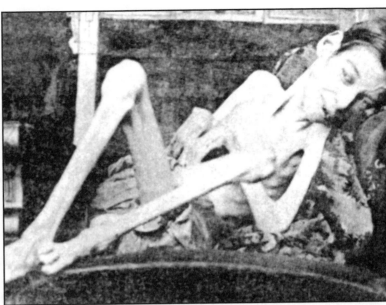

Pete Robinson

Rosa Lee Plemons

Famous fat ladies – much more traditional in show business than their male counterparts – have included: Miss Bertha (415 pounds), Olga, Anna (542 pounds aged 18), Victorine, Flossie, Marie Lill, Celeste Geyer (born 1901, better known as Dolly Dimples, who once weighed 500 pounds), Baby

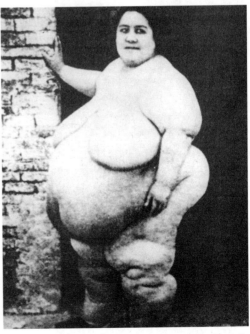

Miss Bertha

Dolly Dimples

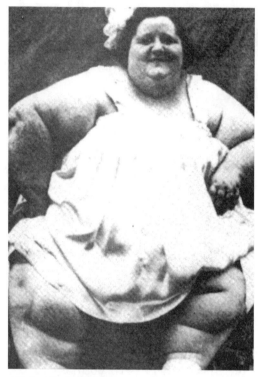

Baby Ruth Pontico

Terresina

Alice from Dallas

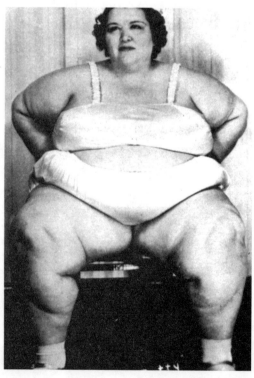

Baby Betty

Daniel Lambert and gravestone

Ruth Pontico (1904-1941, said to weigh 814 pounds), Miss Susan Barton (Barnum's "Mammoth Lady"), Mademoiselle Rose (600 pounds), Jenny Letto, Teresina (star of the Gallery of Monsters at the Neuilly Fair, 583 pounds), Baby Irene, Baby Betty, Baby Thelma (655 pounds), Jolly Josephine, Alice From Dallas, the Canadian Miss Miranda, the Dutchwoman Juliana Voort, and the American negresses Lucy Morris, Flora Mae "Baby Flo" Jackson (840 pounds), "Captivatin'" Liza, and Miss Jean Hill (500-pound star of John Waters' *Desperate Living* [1977]).

Amongst the fattest men recorded in history have been: the Englishmen Nickolas Wood of Kent, Jack Biggers of Witney, Edward Bright of Maldon (584 pounds), and Daniel Lambert of Leicester (1770-1809, 739 pounds); the Americans Johnny Alee (an alleged 1,000 pounds) and Mills Darden (1799-1857, again an alleged 1,000 pounds); Emil Naucke (born 1855, 518 pounds), John Hanson Craig (1856-94, 745 pounds), Wilhelm Loter, the Cannon Colossus, William J. "Happy Humphrey" Cobb (802 pounds), William Campbell, Leo Whitton, John McDonald, and "Happy" Jack Eckert (1877-

Robert Earl Hughes (at age 25)

1939, 739 pounds). Eckert was one of the "Six Tiny Rosebuds", a conglomorate
of show fat-folk from 1938-1939 which also included Baby Thelma, Jolly
Josephine, Tiny Griffin, and Dolly Dimples. The fattest man to have been
medically authenticated remains the American Robert Earl Hughes (1926-58)
of Fish Hook, Illinois. Some ten feet four inches around the waist, Hughes fell

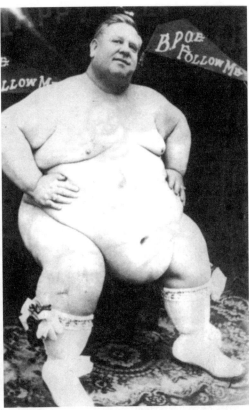

Cannon Colossus

Happy Jack Eckert

ill with measles at the age of 32. Too big for an ambulance, he was driven to hospital in a trailer and treated on the hospital forecourt. He died soon afterwards, and was buried in a piano-case. His weight at death was 1,069 pounds.

Hermaphrodites, and other sexual anomalies

The most coveted, and covert, carnival attractions have always been so-called 'sexual freaks'.[4] Though transsexual surgery can now create hermaphrodites – a male and female in the same body – the authenticity of such 'natural-born' creatures remains in doubt. These androgynous marvels have always figured in classical mythology, but most carnival hermaphrodites ("half-and-halfs") are deemed to have been fakes, despite being perennial crowd-pullers. These 'morphodites' were usually divided laterally, such as Josephine-Joseph who appears in *Freaks*. Others have included Albert-Alberta (aka Bobby Kork from New Jersey), Mary Casey, Benny Rogers, and Donald-Diane.

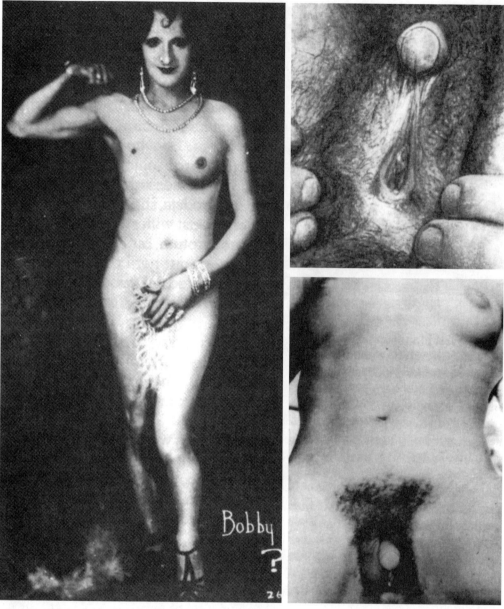

Bobby Kork   *Unknown hermaphrodites*

   Some women have been born with virtually no breasts and a clitoris
so over-developed as to resemble a vestigial penis; others with neither ovaries
nor testicles, but a sterile combination of the two. Neither can be classed as
'fully-functional' hermaphrodites. Nearer to true hermaphrodism are males
with the chromosomal dysfunction Klinefelter's Syndrome (who display

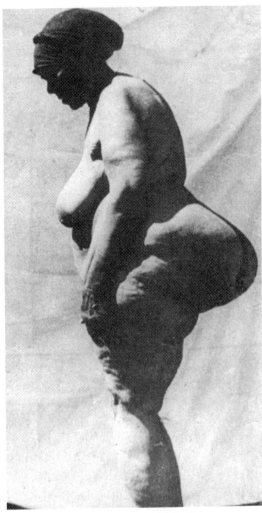

African hermaphrodite   *Hottentot woman*

female breasts and small genitals); these correspond to females with Turner's Syndrome (web-necked, dwarfed, flat-chested). Other genital anomalies have included men with two penises or three testicles, less fortunates with only one testicle ('monorchids') or even none ('eunuchs'), and women with two vaginas. Hypospadias, a condition where the urethral opening is situated on the underside of the penis, can result in deformity of the glans. Related conditions include double or multiple urethral ducts, paired median raphe ducts (causing 'tunnels' in the skin), and even single dorsal ducts. Priapism – a psychotic disorder resulting in permanent erection – was once thought to indicate a boned penis.

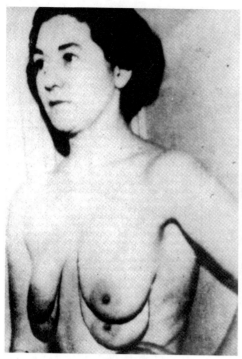

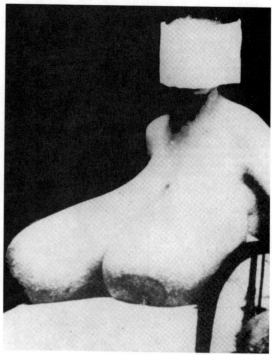

Unidentified woman   *Unidentified woman*

Women have also been reported as possessing a third, or 'supernumerary' nipple – once regarded as the sign of a witch – a complete third breast, or a second or even third set of breasts. Anne Boleyn, besides having six fingers on each hand, is reputed to have had three breasts arranged in a triangle. In 1894, the case of a *man* with no less than six extra nipples was reported; men have also been said to give milk. Certain races of women, such as the Hottentots, are fabled not only for their hyper-extended buttocks, but for labia which dangle down between their thighs.

Finally, the most basic aberration – that of excessive size – made both overly buxotic women and exceptionally 'well-endowed' men much sought-after for an institution which went far beyond what the closely-monitored sideshows had to offer: the stag-movie (forerunner of today's hardcore porno flick). Since its inception, the moving film has always drawn on sideshow tradition in this way, only to eclipse and, ultimately, supersede it. The tradition of using freaks in cinema originated early on in the history of film, with dwarfs being the most common participants[5] – hardly surprising, since it was from the very institution of the freakshow itself that cinema first developed.

Left: Abnormal penis size (natural)
Above centre: Elephantiasis of the scrotum
Above right: Elephantiasis of the penis

NOTES

1. The legend of the feral child is closely linked to that of the "Missing Link", the creature who supposedly embodies the evolutionary stage between ape and man. Lucien Malson's *Wolf Children And The Problem Of Human Nature*, was an account published in 1964 listing some 53 attested cases of this phenomenon.

2. Grady Stiles hit the headlines much more recently, when he was shot four times in the head on November 29, 1992 as he sat watching TV in his Gibsonton trailer. His wife, Mary Teresa Stiles, was later convicted of paying one Christopher Wyant $1,500 to kill Grady who had become a violent drunk prone to beating her savagely with his claws.

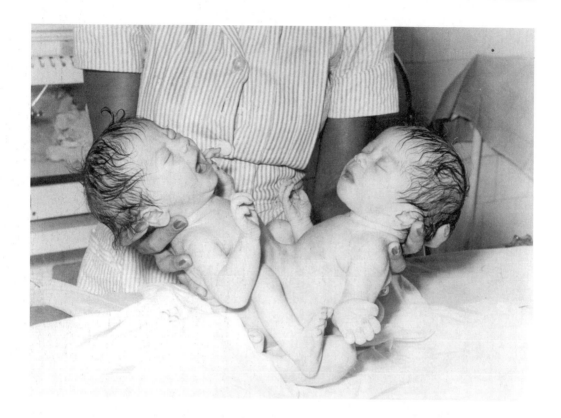

3. Clara and Altagracia (Alta) Rodriguez were born in San José de Ochoa, Dominican Republic, on August 12, 1973. They were ischiopagus twins, joined together at the lower trunk and pelvis. They were separated by Dr. C. Everett Koop at the Children's Hospital of Philadelphia in an eight-hour surgery. Sadly, one year after the separation of the two sisters, Alta choked to death on a bean. Clara survived to maturity.

4. In Freudian terms, it is the onset of puberty – the very sexualization of the child – with its physical distortions, which can first give rise to notions of the 'freakish'; while the increasingly obvious differences between male and female anatomy may instigate our permanent dread of (and fascination with) the 'other' (hence Freud's equivalence of notions of the 'uncanny' with castration/lack).

5. For example *The Haunted Curiosity Shop* (1901); *The Dwarf's Cake Walk* (1905); and *Barnum's Trunk* (1904), which used show-people direct from the circus.

THREE:
TARTARUS

Advent of Cinema • Man-Made Freaks (War: Bad Science: Body Modification)

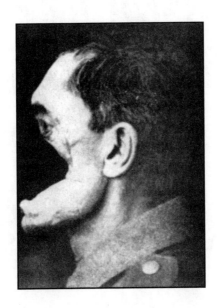

Even before the great Barnum show of 1901, Paris in the 1890s had been gripped by a passion for extravagant theatre; the Grand Guignol, which opened in 1897, live beasts and, indeed, circus freaks were the vogue. At the *Theatre de la Gaité* or the *Varieté* of the time, for instance, the crowds could marvel at the naked dancing girl Bob Walter gyrating behind a mass of snarling beasts, see the deadly Spider-Woman, Mlle Fougère, or witness the most famous Siamese twins in all the world, Rosa-Josepha Blazek. Paris even had its very own "Giants' Restaurant", where visiting goliaths were exhibited while prostitutes plied their trade.

At the same time, another burgeoning branch of the spectacular was about to reach fruition. Throughout the century, various experimenters had been investigating the phenomenon of the persistence of vision, developing ways to give the illusion of moving images either in the name of science, or in order to even further enhance their shows: Dr. John Ayrton Paris' Thaumatrope (1826), Joseph Plateau's Phenakistiscope and Simon

Stampfer's Stroboscope (1833), William George Horner's Zoetrope (1834), Henry R. Heyl's Phasmatrope (1870), Emile Reynaud's Praxinoscope (1877) and his subsequent *Pantomimes Lumineuses*, Eadward Muybridge's Zoopraxiscope (1881), and finally Robert W. Paul's Theatrograph, Thomas Edison's Vitascope and Kinetoscope, Emil Skladanowsky's Bioscop, and the Lumière Brothers' Cinématographe (1895); all had their place in the development of moving pictures. It was this progression of invention which eventually gave birth to the cinematic arts in the mid-1890s. And naturally enough, the first experiments in film would often, in true sideshow fashion, centre around shocking images of the human body – executions, train wrecks, and of course clandestine pornography.

It was during these formative years, at the height of the carnival craze, that a certain Georges Méliès, not content with producing mere documentary footage, was busily developing his pioneering "cinema of magic and illusion". Méliès was himself originally a magician in the music-halls and

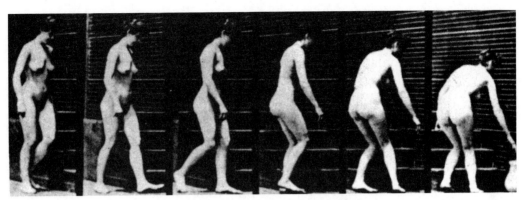

Moving sequence of nude model by Eadward Muybridge, 1901

fairgrounds. In 1887, aged 26, he purchased the legendary Theatre Robert-Houdin, where he had served his sorcerer's apprenticeship. For 8 years he ran the theatre, presenting breath-taking spectacles of sensational tricker – and then he discovered the camera. The Lumière Brothers, operating the first screening-room beneath the Grand Café, were already drawing over two thousand people a day to view their short, documentary-type films. When Méliès began to make films in 1895 (having customised his own camera and projector), he soon grew bored with 'real-life' subjects, and realized that the best effects could be achieved *within* the camera, rather than in the events being filmed; over the next few years his magician's mind would lead him to investigate every conceivable manner of trick photography, single-handedly pioneering the fantasy film genre.

Distortion of the human body was naturally one of the first tricks he developed; in one famous sequence from *The India Rubber Head* (1902), his own head was enlarged to a gigantic size and then exploded. His many other films of illusion and thrills, ranging from *The Laboratory Of Mephistopheles* (1897) and *Apres Le Bal – Le Tub* (1897, often cited as the first 'nudie' film) to *A Trip To The Moon* (1902), *Le Monstre* (1903) and *An Impossible Voyage* (1904), were chiefly exhibited by his friends and associates, the fairground showmen. While his competitors – the Lumière Brothers and Edison and Pathé and Eclair – used theatrical outlets, Méliès trusted to the oldest exhibition pitch of all – the booth in a circus or sideshow.

The very origins of the cinema of imagination are thus intertwined with the tradition of using a sideshow to exhibit freaks and other wonders. And not only were the first films shown in the fairs, but one of the first genuine film classics chose the fairground as its sinister *mise-en-scène*; Robert Wiene's *Cabinet Of Dr. Caligari* (1919) is regarded as the highpoint of German Expressionism, a movement which made many contributions to bizarre cinema. Not least of the film's primary tropes was the carnival setting itself, with its voyeuristic ramifications reminding the viewer of his own participation in the whole cinematic process – a key element in all 'freakshow' films.

Lead actors Conrad Veidt and Werner Krauss also appeared in Paul Leni's highly expressionistic *Das Wachsfigurenkabinett / Waxworks* (1924). In the latter, a poet visits the wax museum at a sinister fairground; in the most frightening of three episodes, remarkable for their outlandish architecture, the figure of Jack the Ripper (Krauss) comes to life and pursues the man and his girlfriend through the night. Arthur Robison's *Schatten / Warning Shadows* (1924) is also of interest: an atmospheric arabesque of macabre shadows, mirrors and reflections, telling of people driven to act out their own secret desires by a stage illusionist. These films are a strong indicator of cinema's origins in, and ties to, the sidehow tradition.

Of all directors working in Hollywood during the '20s and '30s, one in particular will always be associated with the fairground or travelling carnival and its darker aspects. Although best known for *Freaks* (1932), which would prove to be the thematic and artistic summation – and financial and critical ruin – of his career {see Appendix Two], Tod Browning left a remarkable legacy of films set in a similar, dark milieu. The carnival was in Browning's blood from an early age; he ran away from home in his teens and joined a travelling show, performing as half of acts called "The Lizard and the Crow" and the "Hypnotic Living Corpse". His Hollywood apprenticeship began with serving as D.W. Griffith's assistant on *Intolerance* (1916), after which he graduated to direct a string of undistinguished comedies and thrillers before meeting up with the actor who would help shape the darker visions to come – the 'man of a thousand faces', Lon Chaney. Chaney, who would make his name by playing characters of extreme ugliness or physical impairment, had a remarkable background which might even have provided a storyline for one of Tod Browning's films. He was raised by deaf-mute parents; his first wife became alcoholic and burned out her own vocal chords with poison; he then left her for a chorus-girl who was already married to a man with no legs.

Chaney very quickly made a reputation for himself playing grotesque, contorted characters, such as the feral, half-simian freak in *A Blind Bargain* (1922). His first two films with Browning were mediocre, but after Chaney had accomplished his first major screen portrayal of deformity in *The Hunchback Of Notre Dame* (1923), the pair made *The Unholy Three* (1925), a sideshow tale based on the novel *Three Freaks* by Tod Robbins in which Chaney plays Echo, a larcenous ventriloquist who, bored by the carnival and its paltry rewards, devises a rip-off scheme with two of his circus cohorts. With its use of real-life midget Harry Earles, carnival connections and grotesque moments, *The Unholy Three* was very much a warm-up for Browning's later, more *outré* works in that area.

Next came two collaborations with Chaney: *The Blackbird* (1926), in which Chaney once more played a fake cripple, and then the pair's most extreme entry together yet: *The Unknown* (1927). For this story, Browning devised for Chaney his most freakish role to date; as he himself said of the film: "When I work on a story for Chaney, I never think of the plot. That writes itself when I know the characters. *The Unknown* comes simply from the fact that I had an idea about an armless man. So I asked myself what were the most surprising situations and acts which a man as mutilated as that could be involved in. A circus artist who used his feet just as well as his hands, who lost the woman he loved and tried to commit a terrible murder with his toes, that was the result of my speculations."

This was the wild plot to result from Browning's speculations, a sado-masochistic tale of *amour fou* which André Breton himself might have written (the Surrealists reputedly worshipped Browning); the fact that it proved successful – despite being described by one outraged reviewer as "a fiendish mingling of bloodlust, cruelty and horrors" – was both a tribute to the sympathy Chaney could invoke from an audience, and to the ready familiarity of the public with such people and events in fairgrounds and carnivals. And while circus freaks could be glimpsed in various other films of the genre such *Wheel Of Destiny* (1927), *Two Flaming Youths* (also 1927), and *The Sideshow* (1928), none of these works approached the lurid perversity purveyed by Browning.

Chaney followed up *The Unknown* with a double role, again in excruciating make-up, in Browning's *London After Midnight* (also 1927), a pseudovampire tale; and in Browning's *West Of Zanzibar* (1928) he played a sadistic, wheelchair-bound magician. Their remaining projects together, save for a sound remake of *The Unholy Three* in 1930, are less remarkable; Chaney died of throat cancer just after this last film was completed. Browning went on to make his most successful film, Universal's *Dracula* (1931) with Bela Lugosi, but not before he had presented yet another tribute to carnival life – *The Show* (1927). Centred around a Palace of Illusions sideshow, this film featured John Gilbert as a John the Baptist who is 'decapitated' nightly on stage after the dance of Salome (Renée Adorée). A jealous rival attempts to cut off Gilbert's head for real, while the entrance money of the Palace's patrons is seemingly collected by Cleopatra'a severed hand – another recurring and powerful 'horror' film icon. The potency of this disembodied appendage, its ability to breed anxiety, is as harbinger of an amputee zone, the negative space surrounding a bleeding stump. "Dismembered limbs, a severed head, a hand cut off at the wrist... all of these have something particularly uncanny about them," says Freud in his essay "The Uncanny", going on to indeed specify that uncanniness is a feeling closely linked to fear of castration. It certainly appears to have been the driving force behind the pathological morbidity of Browning's cinematic visions. The presence of a legless 'half-girl' further underscores his obsession (fetish?) with amputation and loss (phallic or otherwise), while the film almost incidentally demonstrates the circular links between cinema, theatre and fairground.

Browning's other films concerning the tricks and illusions of the sideshow included *The Mystic* (1925) and *The Thirteenth Chair* (1929), but it was not until the phenomenal success of *Dracula* that he found himself in a strong enough position to make the ultimate carnival/deformity film: *Freaks* a true masterpiece of exploitation cinema [see appendix].

As cinema continued its ascendence and developed its facility to portray the fantastic, interest in sideshows began to wane almost in direct ratio; in cinema, both mainstream and underground, darker and stranger marvels could be created for view. Advances in medicine were also reducing the number of 'freak' births, and the public's growing sophistication was leading them both to scorn the ever-increasing ratio of obvious self-mades and fakes ("grifts"), and to frown more and more upon the 'exploitation' of those unfortunate enough to have genuinely slipped through Nature's net. The freakshow was being marginalised. More crucially, a preponderance of global atrocities was accruing which would eventually outstrip even the worst horrors dreamt up by the cinema; through war, drugs, and radiation, man was about to supersede Nature once and for all in his seemingly limitless capacity for the twisting and destruction of human flesh.

The liberation of the Nazi death-camps finally revealed the true horrors of war. Whereas the limbless, the faceless and the broken insane of World War I had been largely shielded from the world's gaze – save for a few isolated anti-war statements such as Ernst Friedrich's protest book *War Against War!* (1925) or Abel Gance's 1938 remake of *J'Accuse!*[1] – the systematic extermination of not only the Jews but also the physically or mentally impaired in the ovens of Auschwitz, Belsen and the other death camps could not be ignored. Singling out such people, even if only to ogle at in sideshows, was nonetheless the first step necessary to eradicate them. In this sense, the carnivals – and their patrons – were perceived to be as guilty of persecution as Hitler and his cohorts. The Nazis banned freakshows in 1937, thereby enabling 'freaks' to be arrested and incarcerated as 'useless people'; their 'Degenerate Art' exhibition damned most modern art, proclaiming it could only be the work of the mentally or physically retarded[2]; while Hitler (whose favourite movie, ironically was reportedly Disney's *Snow White And The Seven Dwarfs*!) instigated the mass cremation of anyone and everyone displaying such aberrations. And then there were the experiments.

Dr Josef Mengele not only had the blessings of the Führer, but also found validation for his activities in the eugenics and cloning theories of Dr Etienne Wolff[3] of the University of Strasbourg, as well as other 'experimental teratologists'. Mengele's alleged skin lampshades and curtains were merely the trimmings on an ongoing quest to hybridise and homogenise, his sadistic surgical practises – almost a real-life parody of '30s Hollywood horror movies like *Island Of Lost Souls*, with its House of Pain – resulting in the most hellish atrocities. With Auschwitz as his hermetic empire, Mengele had suddenly found himself with the absolute power over life and death; like the mad Romans, he also indulged himself by collecting human oddities and became known by the epithet "The Freak Hunter". Dwarfs were his favourite, particularly hunchbacks, although he also favoured cretins and imbeciles. There was even a resident portrait artist at Auschwitz whose task was to preserve the features of dwarfs on canvas, before their inevitable trip to the ovens. Others, such as the severely deformed osteomalaciac Alexander Kalan, were photographed first in life, and then in death – the flesh stripped from

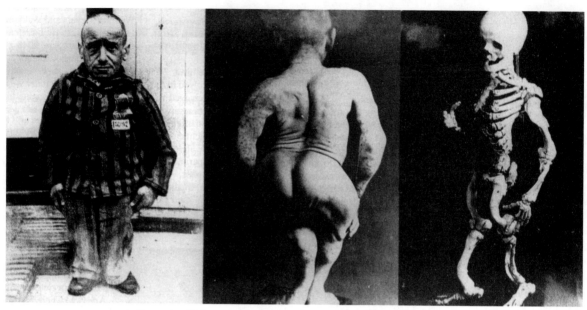

Alexander Kalan, victim of Josef Mengele, in three stages of death

their bones. But Mengele's greatest obsession was with twins, upon whom he conducted endless tests and experiments. These included inter-breeding projects, the making of monsters. Though twins were generally treated better than other prisoners for this reason, Mengele would often kill one of a pair on a whim for immediate autopsy; the simultaneous execution of twin siblings was another favourite pastime. One report has him killing and dissecting fourteen twins in one night. Arbitrary castrations and other mutilations were commonplace.

Mengele's other area of interest involved facial deformity and characteristics. As well as studying noma – a gangrenous condition of the face occurring frequently in Gypsy children – he conducted intense research into eye colour, especially heterochromia (where a person has one blue and one brown eye). He was especially outraged at those who had blond hair yet brown eyes, and would inject their eyeballs with searing chemicals in an attempt to turn them an Aryan blue. Jars of Gypsy eyeballs, rows of severed heads and other anatomical ephemera proliferated his laboratories.

In direct contrast to the crematorial pall over frozen Europe, yet equally maiming to the human spirit, came the blinding nova heat as Hiroshima burnt in a nuclear firestorm. It is difficult to speculate on the level of guilt felt by Americans on a conscious level over the thousands of Japanese men, women and children reduced to seared raw meat in burns units, or the mutant children which would issue from the irradiated genes of the survivors over the next generations,[4] but on a subconscious level at least it must have contributed to the post-atomic angst which epitomised American life – and by extension its pop/pulp cinema (*cf.* Robert Aldrich's *Kiss Me Deadly* [1955]) – over the ensuing decades. Future events would only compound the constant feeling of futility and vague but omnipresent threat to 'normal' ways of life. The sideshow freaks, once primal ciphers reminding us of our darker nature, were no longer required; the true horrors of man's inhumanity to man were for evermore exposed for all to see.

As the century progresed, science also had a role to play in the making of human anomalies. In 1961 a new, supposedly safe tranquillizer for the relief of morning sickness in pregnant women was made available – thalidomide. The drug, however, affected fetal development, and in forty-six countries women who had trustingly taken this virulent teratogen gave birth to profoundly deformed babies. Babies without limbs, without eyes, without mouths, without anuses, without viscera, without *brains*. The phocomelians we have come to associate with the drug represent only the tip of the iceberg; they were the ones (un)lucky enough to survive, to be equipped for some form of life. Indeed, the following description of a typical thalidomide infant, taken from the book *Suffer The Children*, reads like nothing so much as a blueprint for the nightmare foetus/baby of David Lynch's *Eraserhead*: "*He had a deformed and shortened arm and a hand without a thumb. The other hand had one extra finger. His palate had a gaping hole in it. His face was paralyzed on one side. One ear was completely missing, the other grossly deformed. For the first eighteen months of his life, he vomited his food across the room with projectile-like force. It soon became clear that his brain was damaged, that he was deaf and dumb.*"[5] Reports such as this filled the international press, replete with horrifying photographs. It was nothing less than a global freakshow, a fist in the face for the hallowed nuclear family, and its eventual repercussions could only serve to increase the demand for suppression of all such ungodly workings and displays.

A few short years later, America compounded this earlier chemical infanticide by sacrificing thousands of its finest young men in a hellish killing arena – Vietnam. The details of that conflict do not need repeating. A generation of wounded returned to their home country as virtual outsiders, shattered and maimed in both mind and body. Meanwhile, the highly toxic US defoliant dioxin Agent Orange has permeated the entire water-table of Vietnam, resulting in two-headed babies and many other freak births even to this day.[6] (In 10 years [1961–1971], the US army used 80 million litres of Agent Orange.)

By the time Tod Browning's *Freaks*, banned for many years, was (partially) rehabilitated in 1962 – ironically at the height of the thalidomide scandal – the sideshow life it depicted was vanishing to a large degree. Though a few die-hards, such as Ward Hall and Whitey Sutton, would persist to the bitter end, most were rolling over. When the shows closed down, the freaks had nowhere to turn, and many of them readily joined an organisation inaugurated by former showman Anton Szandor LaVey in San Francisco in the '60s – The Church of Satan. LaVey had many carnival friends, and knew (side)show business intimately, but summed up the attraction of his sect to the freaks thus: "They feel that God has treated them unfairly by allowing them to be born deformed, and Satan, himself an outcast, has more sympathy for their plight." The Church, which thus heralded Satan as fallen angel rather than devil, a figurehead for rebels against unjust authority, started with few members but very soon grew to have several thousand, including the likes of Sammy Davis Jr, Jayne Mansfield and, latterly, rock band The Eagles (*Hotel California* being, it is said, a reference to the Church's first premises on California street, San Francisco). It still flourishes today, and LaVey's books, such as *The Satanic Bible* and *The Satanic Witch*, are perennial sellers among the disaffected of all classes and professions.

One of the many people who turned on to the revival of *Freaks* was a young New York fashion photographer, Diane Arbus. She became instantly obsessed with the film, or more specifically with its gallery of fascinating human oddities, and went to see it over and over again. Arbus declared that from then on, she would devote herself to cataloguing these near-extinct marvels, to creating a permanent record of the darker, "evil mirror" side of human society and nature. She began seeking out live freaks of her own to capture on film, frequenting such shady haunts as Hubert's Museum on 42nd Street – one of the last existing residential freakshows in America – in her quest. Here she encountered all the traditional sideshow acts, including the famous phocomele Sealo, and the tattooed man Jack Dracula, who boasted no less than 306 illustrations from horror movies on his face, limbs and torso.

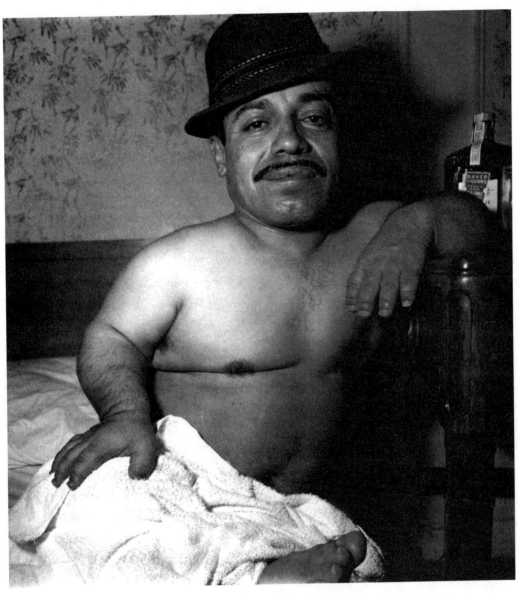

Morales, the Mexican dwarf photographed by Diane Arbus

Other anomalies she photographed regularly included a group of Russian midgets, a Jewish giant called Eddie Carmel, and a Mexican dwarf by name of Morales. Hubert's shut down in 1965; Arbus went after shots of other odd people, such as winos, hardcore Village lesbians, junkies, drag queens, nudists, even identical triplets and twins, but she would always return to her beloved freaks. As she later reflected:

"I just used to adore them. I still do adore some of them. I don't quite

mean they're my best friends but they made me feel a mixture of shame and awe. There's a quality of legend about freaks. Like a person in a fairy tale who stops you and demands that you answer a riddle. Most people go through life dreading they'll have a traumatic experience. Freaks were born with their trauma. They've already passed their test in life. They're aristocrats."[7]

Diane Arbus committed suicide in 1972, by which time the sideshows were all but banished, generally regarded as disgusting anachronisms. This was underlined by a case in 1972, when the North Fair Show (featuring seasoned pros Sealo and dwarf Pete Terhune), tried to pitch in North Bay Village, Florida. Residents brought an injunction, citing an old law by which freakshows were explicitly equated with pornography. Although the case was finally overturned, the message was clear: displaying deformed flesh was now deemed as obscene as showing hardcore sex; the Seal Boy's flippers as forbidden and unwelcome in town by decent folk as a spurting penis, gaping vulva or sodomised anus.

We now have special-effects cinema in place of live freak shows; and indeed, the mutations of John Carpenter's *The Thing*, David Cronenberg's *Videodrome* or Paul Verhoeven's *Total Recall* far surpass anything Mother Nature could ever have concocted. Likewise, the terrible results of years of chemical pollution and radiation leakage – our shameful 'fourth world' of man-made freaks – can never be admitted or revealed by the regimes and corporations responsible. In Brazil – where thalidomide and similar drugs are still prescribed to pregnant women – singer Nick Cave tells of freaks performing in local nightclubs; limbless beggars – usually crippled by their own parents – throng the sub-continent of India; but in the 'progressive' West, such sights are a thing of the past. Despite the homages paid to a nostalgic geek/amputee underworld by *manga* artist Maruo Suehiro in *Mr Arashi's Amazing Freak Show* and by American artist Joe Coleman in such exquisitely repulsive books as *The Mystery Of Wolverine Woo-Bait* (1982) and *Cosmic Retribution* (1992) [Coleman also had a stage act which in 1981 reportedly involved him biting the heads off live mice], and a vain bid by the Jim Rose Circus to reinstate geeking (of sorts) as a pastime fit for mass consumption, the only traces of the old sideshows are locked away in the deathly still of hospitals or museums, teratological refuges such as the Mütter Museum of Pathology, a collection donated to the College of Physicians of Philadelphia in 1858 and augmented ever since. Besides a post-autopsy plastercast of Chang and Eng and their joint liver, this reliquary houses the burnished bones of giants and dwarfs alongside club-footed, cretin and craniopagic skeleta, plus the only known remains of a sufferer from the rare crippling disease Fibrodysplasia Ossificans Progressiva, a condition where surplus bone forms and spreads at random over the normal skeleton, resembling a curtain of molten wax.

Inspired by such very collections is perhaps the only man still carrying on – and indeed far superseding – the darker photographic preoccupations of Diane Arbus. Joel-Peter Witkin's astonishing photographs have been published and exhibited worldwide. His is a body of work as extreme and taboo (and yet strangely erotic) as any in existence; lush, chemically-treated monochrome images of dwarfs, bearded women, amputees, hunchbacks, (especially) hermaphrodites, and any other human oddities that may fall beneath his lens, juxtaposed with props from a black carnival in which medical appliances and prostheses are melded with S/M accoutrements to form a startling atrocity zone. *Leda, Art Deco Lamp, Bacchus Amelus, Picasso En Los Disparates De Goya*: these are just a few dispatches from a catalogue unparalleled in its depictions of a lascivious living Hell.

Not content with these living wonders, Witkin has also transgressed further, working with dead flesh and bone, raiding the necropolis for the body parts used in the composition of such pictures as *Le Baiser* and *The Feast Of Fools*. In this religious quest for the Freudian uncanny, Witkin is clearly a soul in the tradition of not only Diane Arbus, but *Freaks* director Tod Browning himself; in his volume of perversely beautiful portraits, *Gods Of Earth And Heaven*, he proclaims the following manifesto:

"I need physical marvels – a person, thing or act so extraordinary as to inspire wonder: someone with wings, horns, tails, fins, claws, reversed feet, head, hands. Anyone with additional arms, legs, eyes, breasts, genitals, ears, nose, lips, head. Anyone without a face. Pinheads, dwarfs, giants, Satyrs. A woman with one breast (center); a woman with breasts so large as to require Daliesque supports; women whose faces are covered with hair or large skin lesions and willing to pose in evening gowns. Active and retired sideshow performers, contortionists (erotic), anyone with a parasitic twin, people who live as comic book heroes. Boot, corset and bondage fetishists, a beautiful woman with functional appendages in place of arms, anorexics (preferably bald), the romantic and criminally insane (nude only). All manner of extreme

visual perversions. A young blonde girl with two faces. Hermaphrodites and taratoids (alive and dead). Beings from other planets. Anyone bearing the wounds of Christ. Anyone claiming to be God. God.'[8]

The persistence of the art of Joel-Peter Witkin and like-minded others may be seen as indicating the presence of a growing underground resistance to the all-pervasive corporate body-imaging of the '90s, a rebel movement to reclaim the human form by its individual owners. Whereas the demand for real-life ("voyeuristic") freak shows began to decline steadily after the '40s and '50s, the passion for tattooing as a private adornment has grown with equal progress. A similar, more recent increase in body-piercing, not only of ears and noses but also of nipples, genitals and other erogenous areas, has given rise to a trend known as "modern primitivism", where Westerners are willingly undergoing tattooing, piercing, scarification and other body modifications – even self-mutilation – normally thought to be the sole province of Eastern or African tribes, in order to assert an independent control over their personal and private lives. Male and female infibulation, once a punitive or feudal imposition, is now highly desirable. This new ideology is also indubitably reflected by the rising interest in sado-masochistic and fetishistic sex iconography and ritual. The live shows of Californian Ron Athey represent the apex of this new aesthetic. Athey is run through with sharp implements by his heavily tattooed and pierced assistants, his bald head transfixed by a crown of needles; genitals are sewn together, the stage awash with blood by the time the rites have ended.

Hermaphrodites are commonplace due to the wonders of modern surgery, while budding porno starlets have undergone massive silicon implants to augment their bust sizes to unheard-of dimensions in a bid to top the ratings. Penis enlargement is an escalating industry, and many other cosmetic operations – in spite of entailing cutting and slicing more graphic than anything inflicted by the 'psychos' of slasher movies – have become routine. Women are giving men licence to legally inflict upon them the kind of wounds usually perceived as the 'sick' dreams of misogynistic serial killers.

Recent development in medical science – cloning, genetic engineering, stem-cell therapy, "cyborg" techology – also pose the question of whether by advancing in the field of the creation of "designer people", we are in fact regressing to a new "dark age" of man-made freaks (albeit with perfection, rather than mutilation, in mind). In replacing soft body parts with machines, we are heading toward an era of a new kind of freak; not made by nature, or drugs, but by computer science. Not a freak of deformity, but of *conformity*. It remains to be seen whether this craving for physical perfection will yet come full circle and precipitate a millennial backlash that plunges us once more toward the Hellscapes and apocalyptic bestiaries of our unconscious.[9]

In a world of perfect people, difference is the only mark of recognition.

NOTES

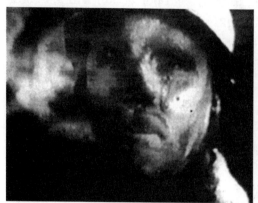

Two disfigured soldiers from "J'Accuse"

1.   In re-making his classic anti-war film, Gance went to exceptional extremes. For the climactic scenes, in which the vengeful war dead rise from their graves to prevent the living from precipitating fresh carnage, Gance employed as actors actual facially disfigured veterans of World War I, recruited from the *Union des Gueules Cassées* (Union of Ruined Faces).

2. When Hitler activated his mass euthanasia/extermination program, Aktion T-4, in October 1939, he declared its first victims should be those "judged incurably sick, by critical medical examination"; what this meant in reality was a mass purging of mental asylums, commencing with those in Poland. SS soldiers of Einsatzkommando 16 first cleared the hospitals and mental asylums of the Wartheland, in western Poland, followed by Danzig and the Gdynia area; these purges alone accounted for the extermination of around 20,000 mentally or physically impaired older children and adults (a decree had already been issued for the culling of all children under the age of three who suffered from idiocy, mongolism, blindness or deafness, microcephaly, hydrocephaly, malformations of limbs, head, or spinal column, and paralysis). At Polsen, hundreds of patients died in improvised gas chambers, anticipating the methods which would eventually be employed in Hitler's next killing program, the Final Solution.

SS photographs of Polish mental asylum inmates, 1930s

3. Wolff's treatise *La Science Des Monstres* was eventually published by Gallimard (Paris, 1948).

4. One report in *Medical News* stated that: *"Examination of children born in Nagasaki since 1945 reveals an enormous increase in deformities. The damage is lasting, because the origin of the defects is a change in the reproductive cells of all the inhabitants affected by radiation, a change that is inherited and cannot be reversed. Of 30,150 children examined, 3,630 have serious defects, which may be classified as follows:– 1,046 children: degeneration of the bones, muscles, skin, and nervous system; 429: deformities of the organs of sight or hearing; 254: hare-lips or tongue deformities; 59: lung deformities; 47: jaw deformities; 25: born without brains; 8: born without eyes or eye-sockets."*

5. The Insight Team of *The Times* of London; *Suffer The Children: The Story Of Thalidomide* (New York: The Viking Press, 1979), p.112.

6. The following, for example, is from a recent account of two reporters in South Vietnam: *"The reporters made the trip to a hospital called "peace hospital", where they were shown to two wards. The first one was a big room with shelves of formaldehyde-filled jars containing deformed fetuses. The grotesque image underlies the importance of banning the usage of chemical or biological weapons under any circumstances, because of their long-term devastating impact on the most vulnerable members of our society: the kids.*

"Among the living kids in the other ward, they saw kids with huge Martian-like eye-balls, who can not ever close their eyes, kids with heads bigger than their bodies, others with hands having only 2 crab-claw-like fingers, and more mentally impaired. One kid, whom medical personnel cannot identifiy as male or female, had a face without eyes entirely, the result of the failure for the eye crack to develop during the fetus stage. 'I don't know what to say,' one of the reporters Xiao Ma commented. 'It's a bloody living hell, with nowhere to hide or escape.'"

7. Arbus, Diane; *Photographs* (New York: Aperture Books, 1972).

8. Witkin, Joel-Peter; *Gods Of Earth And Heaven* (California: Twelve Trees Press, 1989).

9. Already, body modification mania has led some to disturbing new extremes in this direction, with individuals turning themselves into half-human, half-beasts such as the "lizard-man" and the "cat-man" which directly recall the old freakshow terminologies.

APPENDIX ONE:
"THE ELEPHANT MAN"
by
Sir Frederick Treves

A True Account
first published in 1923

In the Mile End Road, opposite to the London Hospital, there was (and possibly still is) a line of small shops. Among them was a vacant greengrocer's which was to let. The whole of the front of the shop, with the exception of the door, was hidden by a hanging sheet of canvas on which was the announcement that the "Elephant Man" was to be seen within and that the price of admission was two-pence. Painted on the canvas in primitive colours was a life-size portrait of the Elephant Man. This very crude production depicted a frightful creature that could only have been possible in a nigh mare. It was the figure of a man with the characteristics of a elephant. The transfiguration was not far advanced. There was still more of the man than of the beast. This fact – that it was still human – was the most repellent attribute of the creature. There was nothing about it of the pitiableness of the misshapened or the deformed, nothing of the grotesqueness of the freak, but merely the loathsome insinuation of a man being changed into an animal. Some palm trees in the background of the picture suggested a jungle and might have Ied the imaginative to assume that it was in this wild that the perverted object had roamed.

When I first became aware of this phenomenon the exhibition was closed, but a well-informed boy sought the proprietor in a public house and I was granted a private view on payment of a shilling. The shop was empty and grey with dust. Some old tins and a few shrivelled potatoes occupied shelf and some vague vegetable refuse the window. The light in the place was dim, being obscured by the painted placard outside. The far end of the shop — where I expect the late proprietor sat at a desk — was cut off by a curtain or rather by red tablecloth suspended from a cord by a few rings. The room was cold and dank, for it was the month of November. The year, I might say, was 1884.

The showman pulled back the curtain and revealed a bent figure crouching on a stool and covered by a brown blanket. In front of it, on a tripod, was a large brick heated by a Bunsen burner. Over this the creature was huddled to warm itself. It never moved when the curtain was drawn back. Locked up in an empty shop and lit by the faint blue light of the gas jet, this hunched-up figure was the embodiment of loneliness. It might have been a captive in a cavern or a wizard watching for unholy manifestations in the ghostly flame. Outside the sun was shining and one could hear the footsteps of the passers-by, a tune whistled by a boy and the companionable hum of traffic in the road.

The showman — speaking as if to a dog — called out harshly: 'Stand up!' The thing arose slowly and let the blanket that covered its head and back fall to the ground. There stood revealed the most disgusting specimen of humanity that I have ever seen. In the course of my profession I had come upon lamentable deformities of the face due to injury or disease, as well as mutilations and contortions of the body depending upon like causes; but at no time had I met with such a degraded or perverted version of a human being as this lone figure displayed. He was naked to the waist, his feet were bare, he wore a pair of threadbare trousers that had once belonged to some fat gentleman's dress suit.

From the intensified painting in the street I had imagined the Elephant Man to be of gigantic size. This, however, was a little man below the average height and made to look shorter by the bowing of his back. The most striking feature about him was his enormous and misshapened head. From the brow there projected a huge bony mass like a loaf, while from the back of the head hung a bag of spongy, fungous-looking skin, the surface of which was comparable to brown cauliflower. On the top of the skull were a few long lank hairs. The osseous growth on the forehead almost occluded one eye. The circumference of the head was no less than that of the man's waist. From the upper jaw there projected another mass of bone. It protruded from the mouth like a pink stump, turning the upper lip inside out and making of the mouth a mere slobbering aperture. This growth from the jaw had been so exaggerated in the painting as to appear to be a rudimentary trunk or tusk. The nose was merely a lump of flesh, only recognizable as a nose from its position. The face was no more capable of expression than a block of gnarled wood. The back was horrible, because from it hung, as far down as the middle of the thigh, huge, sack-like masses of flesh covered by the same loathsome cauliflower skin.

The right arm was of enormous size and shapeless. It suggested the limb of the subject of elephantiasis. It was overgrown also with pendent masses of the same cauliflower-like skin. The hand was large and clumsy – a fin or paddle rather than a hand. There was no distinction between the palm and the back. The thumb had the appearance of a radish, while the fingers might have been thick, tuberous roots. As a limb it was almost useless. The other arm was remarkable by contrast. It was not only normal but was, moreover, a delicately shaped limb covered with fine skin and provided with a beautiful hand which any woman might have envied. From the chest hung a bag of the same repulsive flesh. It was like a dewlap suspended from the neck of a lizard. The lower limbs had the characters of the deformed arm. They were unwieldy, dropsical looking and grossly misshapened.

To add a further burden to his trouble the wretched man, when a boy, developed hip disease, which had left him permanently lame, so that he could only walk with a stick. He was thus denied all means of escape from his tormentors. As he told me later, he could never run away. One other feature must be mentioned to emphasize his isolation from his kind. Although he was already repellent enough, there arose from the fungous skin-growth with which he was almost covered a very sickening stench which was hard to tolerate. From the showman I learnt nothing about the Elephant Man, except that he was English, that his name was John Merrick and that he was twenty-one years of age.

As at the time of my discovery of the Elephant Man I was the Lecturer on Anatomy at the Medical College opposite, I was anxious to examine him in detail and to prepare an account of his abnormalities. I therefore arranged with the showman that I should interview his strange exhibit in my room at the college. I became at once conscious of a difficulty. The Elephant Man could not show himself in the streets. He would have been mobbed by the crowd and seized by the police. He was, in fact, as secluded from the world as the Man with the Iron Mask. He had, however, a disguise, although it was almost as startling as he was himself. It consisted of a long black cloak which reached to the ground. Whence the cloak had been obtained I cannot imagine. I had only seen such a garment on the stage wrapped about the figure of a Venetian bravo. The recluse was provided with a pair of bag-like slippers in which to hide his deformed feet. On his head was a cap of a kind that never before was seen. It was black like the cloak, had a wide peak, and the general outline of a yachting cap. As the circumference of Merrick's head was that of a man's waist, the size of this headgear may be imagined. From the attachment of the peak a grey flannel curtain hung in front of the face. In this mask was cut a wide horizontal slit through which the wearer could look out. This costume, worn by a bent man hobbling along with a stick, is probably the most remarkable and the most uncanny that has as yet been designed. I arranged that Merrick should cross the road in a cab, and to insure his immediate admission to the college I gave him my card. This card was destined to play a critical part in Merrick's life.

I made a careful examination of my visitor the result of which I embodied in a paper (*The British Medical Journal*, Dec., 1886, and April, 1890). I made little of the man himself. He was shy, confused, not a little frightened and evidently much cowed. Moreover, his speech was almost unintelligible. The great bony mass that projected from his mouth blurred his utterance and made the articulation of certain words impossible. He returned in a cab to the place of exhibition, and I assumed that I had seen the last of him, especially as I found next day that the show had been forbidden by the police and that the shop was empty.

I supposed that Merrick was imbecile and had been imbecile from birth. The fact that his face was incapable of expression, that his speech was a mere spluttering and his attitude that of one whose mind was void of all emotions and concerns gave grounds for this belief. The conviction was no doubt encouraged by the hope that his intellect was the blank I imagined it to be. That he could appreciate his position was unthinkable. Here was a man in the heyday of youth who was so vilely deformed that everyone he met confronted him with a look of horror and disgust. He was taken about the country to be exhibited as a monstrosity and an object of loathing. He was shunned like a leper, housed like a wild beast, and got his only view of the world from a peephole in a showman's cart. He was, moreover, lame, had but one available arm, and could hardly make his utterances understood. It was not until I came to know that Merrick was highly intelligent, that he possessed an acute sensibility and – worse than all – a romantic imagination that I realized the overwhelming tragedy of his life.

The episode of the Elephant Man was, I imagined, closed; but I was fated to meet him again two years later – under more dramatic conditions. In England the showman and Merrick had been moved on from place to place by the police, who considered the exhibition degrading and among the things that could not be allowed. It was hoped that in the uncritical retreats of Mile End a more abiding peace would be found. But it was not to be. The official mind there, as elsewhere, very properly decreed that the public exposure of Merrick and his deformities transgressed the limits of decency. The show must close.

The showman, in despair, fled with his charge to the Continent. Whither he roamed at first I do not know; but he came finally to Brussels. His reception was discouraging. Brussels was firm; the exhibition was banned; it was brutal, indecent and immoral, and could not be permitted within the confines of Belgium. Merrick was thus no longer of value. He was no longer a source of profitable entertainment. He was a burden. He must be got rid of. The elimination of Merrick was a simple matter. He could offer no resistance. He was as docile as a sick sheep. The impresario, having robbed Merrick of his paltry savings, gave him a ticket to London, saw him into the train and no doubt in parting condemned him to perdition.

His destination was Liverpool Street. The journey may be imagined. Merrick was in his alarming outdoor garb. He would be harried by an eager mob as he hobbled along the quay. They would run ahead to get a look at him. They would lift the hem of his cloak to peep at his body. He would try to hide in the train or in some dark corner of the boat, but never could he be free from that ring of curious eyes or from those whispers of fright and aversion. He had but a few shillings in his pocket and nothing either to eat or drink on the way. A panic-dazed dog with a label on his collar would have received some sympathy and possibly some kindness. Merrick received none.

What was he to do when he reached London? He had not a friend in the world. He knew no more of London than he knew of Peking. How could he find a lodging, or what lodging-house keeper would dream of taking him in? All he wanted was to hide. What most he dreaded were the open street and the gaze of his fellow-men. If even he crept into a cellar the horrid eyes and the still more dreaded whispers would follow him to its depths. Was there ever such a homecoming!

At Liverpool Street he was rescued from the crowd by the police and taken into the third-class waiting-room. Here he sank on the floor in the darkest corner. The police were at a loss what to do with him. They had dealt with strange and mouldy tramps, but never with such an object as this. He could not explain himself. His speech was so maimed that he might as well have spoken in Arabic. He had, however, something with him which he produced with a ray of hope. It was my card.

The card simplified matters. It made it evident that this curious creature had an acquaintance and that the individual must be sent for. A messenger was dispatched to the London Hospital which is comparatively near at hand. Fortunately I was in the building and returned at once with the messenger to the station. In the waiting-room I had some difficulty in making a way through the crowd, but there, on the floor in the corner, was Merrick. He looked a mere heap. It seemed as if he had been thrown there like a bundle. He was so huddled up and so helpless looking that he might have had both his arms and his legs broken. He seemed pleased to see me, but he was nearly done. The journey and want of food had reduced him to the last stage of exhaustion. The police kindly helped him into a cab, and I drove him at once to the hospital. He appeared to be content, for he fell asleep almost as soon as he was seated and slept to the journey's end. He never said a word, but seemed to be satisfied that all was well.

In the attics of the hospital was an isolation ward with a single bed. It was used for emergency purposes – for a case of delirium tremens, for a man who had become suddenly insane or for a patient with an undetermined fever. Here the Elephant Man was deposited on a bed, was made comfortable and was supplied with food. I had been guilty of an irregularity in admitting such a case, for the hospital was neither a refuge nor a home for incurables. Chronic cases were not accepted, but only those requiring active treatment, and Merrick was not in need of such treatment. I applied to the sympathetic chairman of the committee, Mr. Carr Gomm, who not only was good enough to approve my action but who agreed with me that Merrick must not again be turned out into the world.

Mr. Carr Gomm wrote a letter to *The Times* detailing the circumstances of the refugee and asking for money for his support. So generous is the English public that in a few days I think in a week – enough money was forthcoming to maintain Merrick for life without any charge upon the hospital funds. There chanced to be two empty rooms at the back of the hospital which were little used. They were on the ground floor, were out of the way, and opened upon a large courtyard called Bedstead Square, because here the iron beds were marshalled for cleaning and painting. The front room was converted into a bed-sitting room and the smaller chamber into a bathroom. The condition of Merrick's skin rendered a bath at least once a day a necessity, and I might here mention that with the use of the bath the unpleasant odour to which I have referred ceased to be noticeable. Merrick took up his abode in the hospital in December, 1886.

Merrick had now something he had never dreamed of, never supposed to be possible – a home of his own for life. I at once began to make myself acquainted with him and to endeavour to understand his mentality. It was a study of much interest. I very soon learnt his speech so that I could talk freely with him. This afforded him great satisfaction, for, curiously enough, he had a passion for conversation, yet all his life had had no one to talk to. I – having then much leisure -saw him almost every day, and made a point of spending some two hours with him every Sunday morning when he would chatter almost without ceasing. It was unreasonable to expect one nurse to attend to him continuously, but there was no lack of temporary volunteers. As they did not all acquire his speech it came about that I had occasionally to act as an interpreter.

I found Merrick, as I have said, remarkably intelligent. He had learnt to read and had become a most voracious reader. I think he had been taught when he was in hospital with his diseased hip. His range of books was limited. The Bible and Prayer Book he knew intimately, but he had subsisted for the most part upon newspapers, or rather upon such fragments of old journals as he had chanced to pick up. He had read a few stories and some elementary lesson books, but the delight of his life was a romance, especially a love romance. These tales were very real to him, as real as any narrative in the Bible, so that he would tell them to me as incidents in the lives of people who had lived. In his outlook upon the world he was a child, yet a child with some of the tempestuous feelings of a man. He was an elemental being, so primitive that he might have spent the twenty-three years of his life immured in a cave.

Of his early days I could learn but little. He was very loath to talk about the past. It was a nightmare, the shudder of which was still upon him. He was born, he believed, in or about Leicester. Of his father he knew absolutely nothing. Of his mother he had some memory. It was very faint and had, I think, been elaborated in his mind into something definite. Mothers figured in the tales he had read, and he wanted his mother to be one of those comfortable lullaby-singing persons who are so lovable. In his subconscious mind there was apparently a germ of recollection in which someone figured who had been kind to him. He clung to this conception and made it more real by invention, for since the day when he could toddle no one had been kind to him. As an infant he must have been repellent, although his deformities did not become gross until he had attained his full stature.

It was a favourite belief of his that his mother was beautiful. The fiction was, I am aware, one of his own making, but it was a great joy to him. His mother, lovely as she may have been, basely deserted him when he was very small, so small that his earliest clear memories were of the workhouse to which he had been taken. Worthless and inhuman as this mother was, he spoke of her with pride and even with reverence. Once, when referring to his own appearance, he said: 'It is very strange, for, you see, mother was so beautiful.'

The rest of Merrick's life up to the time that I met him at Liverpool Street Station was one dull record of degradation and squalor. He was dragged from town to town and from fair to fair as if he were a strange beast in a cage. A dozen times a day he would have to expose his nakedness and his piteous deformities before a gaping crowd who greeted him with such mutterings as 'Oh! What a horror! What a beast!' He had had no childhood. He had had no boyhood. He had never experienced pleasure. He knew nothing of the joy of living nor of the fun of things. His sole idea of happiness was to creep into the dark and hide. Shut up alone in a booth, awaiting the next exhibition, how mocking must have sounded the laughter and merriment of the boys and girls outside who were enjoying the 'fun of the fair'! He had no past to look back upon and no future to look forward to. At the age of twenty he was a creature without hope. There was nothing in front of him but a vista of caravans creeping along a road, of rows of glaring show tents and of circles of staring eyes with, at the end, the spectacle of a broken man in a poor law infirmary.

Those who are interested in the evolution of character might speculate as to the effect of this brutish life upon a sensitive and intelligent man. It would be reasonable to surmise that he would become a spiteful and malignant misanthrope, swollen with venom and filled with hatred of his fellow-men, or, on the other hand, that he would degenerate into a despairing melancholic on the verge of idiocy. Merrick, however, was no such being. He had passed through the fire and had come out unscathed. His troubles had ennobled him. He showed himself to be a gentle, affectionate and lovable creature, as amiable as a happy woman, free from any trace of cynicism or resentment, without a grievance and without an unkind word for anyone. I have never heard him complain. I have never heard him deplore his ruined life or resent the treatment he had received at the hands of callous keepers. His journey through life had been indeed along a *via dolorosa*, the road had been uphill all the way, and now, when the night was at its blackest and the way most steep, he had suddenly found himself, as it were, in a friendly inn, bright with light and warm with welcome. His gratitude to those about him was pathetic in its sincerity and eloquent in the childlike simplicity with which it was expressed.

As I learnt more of this primitive creature I found that there were two anxieties which were prominent in his mind and which he revealed to me with diffidence. He was in the occupation of the rooms assigned to him and had been assured that he would be cared for to the end of his days. This, however, he found hard to realize, for he often asked me timidly to what place he would next be moved. To understand his attitude it is necessary to remember that he had been moving on and moving on all his life. He knew no other state of existence. To him it was normal. He had passed from the workhouse to the hospital, from the hospital back to the workhouse, then from this town to that town or from one showman's caravan to another. He had never known a home nor any semblance of one. He had no possessions. His sole belongings, besides his clothes and some books, were the monstrous cap and the cloak. He was a wanderer, a pariah and an outcast. That his quarters at the hospital were his for life he could not understand. He could not rid his mind of the anxiety which had pursued him for so many years — where am I to be taken next?

Another trouble was his dread of his fellow men, his fear of people's eyes, the dread of being always stared at, the lash of the cruel mutterings of the crowd. In his home in Bedstead Square he was secluded; but now and then a thoughtless porter or a ward-maid would open his door to let curious friends have a peep at the Elephant Man. It therefore seemed to him as if the gaze of the world followed him still.

Influenced by these two obsessions he became, during his first few weeks at the hospital, curiously uneasy. At last, with much hesitation, he said to me one day: 'When I am next moved can I go to a blind asylum or to a lighthouse?' He had read about blind asylums in the newspapers and was attracted by the thought of being among people who could not see. The lighthouse had another charm. It meant seclusion from the curious. There at least no one could open a door and peep in at him. There he would forget that he had once been the Elephant Man. There he would escape the vampire showman. He had never seen a lighthouse, but he had come upon a picture of the Eddystone, and it appeared to him that this lonely column of stone in the waste of the sea was such a home as he had longed for.

I had no great difficulty in ridding Merrick's mind of these ideas. I wanted him to get accustomed to his fellow-men, to become a human being himself and to be admitted to the communion of his kind. He appeared day by day less frightened, less haunted looking, less anxious to hide, less alarmed when he saw his door being opened. He got to know most of the people about the place, to be accustomed to their comings and goings, and to realize that they took no more than a friendly notice of him. He could only go out after dark, arid on fine nights ventured to take a walk in Bedstead Square clad in his black cloak and his cap. His greatest adventure was on one moonless evening when he walked alone as far as the hospital garden and back again.

To secure Merrick's recovery and to bring him, as it were, to life once more, it was necessary that he should make the acquaintance of men and women who would treat him as a normal and intelligent young man and not as a monster of deformity. Women I felt to be more important than men in bringing about his transformation. Women were the more frightened of him, the more disgusted at his appearance and the more apt to give way to irrepressible expressions of aversion when they came into his presence. Moreover, Merrick had an admiration of women of such a kind that it attained almost to adoration. This was not the outcome of his personal experience. They were not real women but the products of his imagination. Among them was the beautiful mother surrounded, at a respectful distance, by heroines from the many romances he had read.

His first entry to the hospital was attended by a regrettable incident. He had been placed on the bed in the little attic, and a nurse had been instructed to bring him some food. Unfortunately she had not been fully informed of Merrick's unusual appearance. As she entered the room she saw on the bed, propped up by white pillows, a monstrous figure as hideous as an Indian idol. She at once dropped the tray she was carrying and fled, with a shriek, through the door. Merrick was too weak to notice much, but the experience, I am afraid, was not new to him.

He was looked after by volunteer nurses whose ministrations were somewhat formal and constrained. Merrick, no doubt, was conscious that their service was purely official, that they were merely doing what they were told to do and that they were acting rather as automata than as women.

They did not help him to feel that he was of their kind. On the contrary they, without knowing it, made him aware that the gulf of separation was immeasurable.

Feeling this, I asked a friend of mine, a young and pretty widow, if she thought she could enter Merrick's room with a smile, wish him good morning and shake him by the hand. She said she could and she did. The effect upon poor Merrick was not quite what I had expected. As he let go her hand he bent his head on his knees and sobbed until I thought he would never cease. The interview was over. He told me afterwards that this was the first woman who had ever smiled at him, and the first woman, in the whole of his life, who had shaken hands with him. From this day the transformation of Merrick commenced and he began to change, little by little, from a hunted thing into a man. It was a wonderful change to witness and one that never ceased to fascinate me.

Merrick's case attracted much attention in the papers, with the result that he had a constant succession of visitors. Everybody wanted to see him. He must have been visited by almost every lady of note in the social world. They were all good enough to welcome him with a smile and to shake hands with him. The Merrick whom I had found shivering behind a rag of a curtain in an empty shop was now conversant with duchesses and countesses and other ladies of high degree. They brought him presents, made his room bright with ornaments and pictures, and, what pleased him more than all, supplied him with books. He soon had a large library and most of his day was spent in reading. He was not the least spoiled; not the least puffed up; he never asked for anything; never presumed upon the kindness meted out to him, and was always humbly and profoundly grateful. Above all he lost his shyness. He liked to see his door pushed open and people to look in. He became acquainted with most of the frequenters of Bedstead Square, would chat with them at his window and show them some of his choicest presents. He improved in his speech, although to the end his utterances were not easy for strangers to understand. He was beginning, moreoever, to be less conscious of his unsightliness, a little disposed to think it was, after all, not so very extreme. Possibly this was aided by the circumstance that I would not allow a mirror of any kind in his room.

The height of his social development was reached on an eventful day when Queen Alexandra – then Princess of Wales – came to the hospital to pay him a special visit. With that kindness which has marked every act of her life, the Queen entered Merrick's room smiling and shook him warmly by the hand. Merrick was transported with delight. This was beyond even his most extravagant dream. The Queen has made many people happy, but I think no gracious act of hers has ever caused such happiness as she brought into Merrick's room when she sat by his chair and talked to him as to a person she was glad to see.

Merrick, I may say, was now one of the most contented creatures I have chanced to meet. More than once he said to me: 'I am happy every hour of the day.' This was good to think upon when I recalled the half-dead heap of miserable humanity I had seen in the corner of the waiting-room at Liverpool Street. Most men of Merrick's age would have expressed their joy and sense of contentment by singing or whistling when they were alone. Unfortunately poor Merrick's mouth was so deformed that he could neither whistle nor sing. He was satisfied to express himself by beating time upon the pillow to some tune that was ringing in his head. I have many times found him so occupied when I have entered his room unexpectedly. One thing that always struck me as sad about Merrick was the fact that he could not smile. Whatever his delight might be, his face remained expressionless. He could weep but he could not smile.

The Queen paid Merrick many visits and sent him every year a Christmas card with a message in her own handwriting. On one occasion she sent him a signed photograph of herself. Merrick, quite overcome, regarded it as a sacred object and would hardly allow me to touch it. He cried over it, and after it was framed had it put up in his room as a kind of ikon. I told him that he must write to Her Royal Highness to thank her for her goodness. This he was pleased to do, as he was very fond of writing letters, never before in his life having had anyone to write to. I allowed the letter to be dispatched unedited. It began 'My dear Princess' and ended 'Yours very sincerely'. Unorthodox as it was it was expressed in terms any courtier would have envied.

Other ladies followed the Queen's gracious example and sent their photographs to this delighted creature who had been all his life despised and rejected of men. His mantelpiece and table became so covered with photographs of handsome ladies, with dainty knick-nacks and pretty trifles that they may almost have befitted the apartment of an Adonis-like actor or of a famous tenor.

Through all these bewildering incidents and through the glamour of this great change Merrick still remained in many ways a mere child. He had all the invention of an imaginative boy or girl, the same love of 'make-believe', the same instinct of 'dressing up' and of personating heroic and impressive characters. This attitude of mind was illustrated by the following incident. Benevolent visitors had given me, from time to time, sums of money to be expended for the comfort of the *ci-devant* Elephant Man. When one Christmas was approaching I asked Merrick what he would like me to purchase as a Christmas present. He rather startled me by saying shyly that he would like a dressing-bag with silver fittings. He had seen a picture of such an article in an advertisement which he had furtively preserved.

The association of a silver-fitted dressing-bag with the poor wretch wrapped up in a dirty blanket in an empty shop was hard to comprehend. I fathomed the mystery in time, for Merrick made little secret of the fancies that haunted his boyish brain. Just as a small girl with a tinsel coronet and a window curtain for a train will realize the conception of a countess on her way to court, so Merrick loved to imagine himself a dandy and a young man about town. Mentally, no doubt, he had frequently 'dressed up' for the part. He could 'make-believe' with great effect, but he wanted something to render his fancied character more realistic. Hence the jaunty bag which was to assume the function of the toy coronet and the window curtain that could transform a mite with a pigtail into a countess.

As a theatrical 'property' the dressing-bag was ingenious, since there was little else to give substance to the transformation. Merrick could not wear the silk hat of the dandy nor, indeed, any kind of hat. He could not adapt his body to the trimly cut coat. His deformity was such that he could wear neither collar nor tie, while in association with his bulbous feet the young blood's patent leather shoe was unthinkable. What was there left to make up the character? A lady had given him a ring to wear on his undeformed hand, and a noble lord had presented him with a very stylish walking-stick. But these things, helpful as they were, were hardly sufficing.

The dressing-bag, however, was distinctive, was explanatory and entirely characteristic. So the bag was obtained and Merrick the Elephant Man became, in the seclusion of his chamber, the Piccadilly exquisite, the young spark, the gallant, the 'nut'. When I purchased the article I realized that as Merrick could never travel he could hardly want a dressing-bag. He could not use the silver-backed brushes and the comb because he had no hair to brush. The ivory-handled razors were useless because he could not shave. The deformity of his mouth rendered an ordinary toothbrush of no avail, and as his monstrous lips could not hold a cigarette the cigarette-case was a mockery. The silver shoe-horn would be of no service in the putting on of his ungainly slippers, while the hat-brush was quite unsuited to the peaked cap with its visor.

Still the bag was an emblem of the real swell and of the knockabout Don Juan of whom he had read. So every day Merrick laid out upon his table, with proud precision, the silver brushes, the razors, the show-horn and the silver cigarette-case which I had taken care to fill with cigarettes. The contemplation of these gave him great pleasure, and such is the power of self-deception that they convinced him he was the 'real thing'.

I think there was just one shadow in Merrick's life. As I have already said, he had a lively imagination; he was romantic; he cherished an emotional regard for women and his favourite pursuit was the reading of love stories. He fell in love – in a humble and devotional way – with, I think, every attractive lady he saw. He, no doubt, pictured himself the hero of many a passionate incident. His bodily deformity had left unmarred the instincts and feelings of his years. He was amorous. He would like to have been a lover, to have walked with the beloved object in the languorous shades of some beautiful garden and to have poured into her ear all the glowing utterances that he had rehearsed in his heart. And yet – the pity of it! – imagine the feelings of such a youth when he saw nothing but a look of horror creep over the face of every girl whose eyes met his. I fancy when he talked of life among the blind there was a half-formed idea in his mind that he might be able to win the affection of a woman if only she were without eyes to see.

As Merrick developed he began to display certain modest ambitions in the direction of improving his mind and enlarging his knowledge of the world. He was as curious as a child and as eager to learn. There were so many things he wanted to know and to see. In the first place he was anxious to view the interior of what he called 'a real house', such a house as figured in many of the tales he knew, a house with a hall, a drawing-room where guests were received and a dining-room with plate on the sideboard and with easy chairs into which the hero could 'fling himself'. The workhouse, the common lodging-house and a variety of mean garrets were all the residences he knew. To satisfy this wish I drove him up to my small house in Wimpole Street. He was absurdly interested, and examined everything in detail and with untiring curiosity. I could not show him the pampered menials and the powdered footmen of whom he had read, nor could I produce the white marble staircase of the mansion of romance nor the gilded mirrors and the brocaded divans which belong to that style of residence. I explained that the house was a modest dwelling of the Jane Austen type, and as he had read *Emma* he was content.

A more burning ambition of his was to go to the theatre. It was a project very difficult to satisfy. A popular pantomime was then in progress at Drury Lane Theatre, but the problem was how so conspicuous a being as the Elephant Man could be got there, and how he was to see the performance without attracting the notice of the audience and causing a panic or, at least, an unpleasant diversion. The whole matter was most ingeniously carried through by that kindest of women and most able of actresses – Mrs. Kendal. She made the necessary arrangements with the lessee of the theatre. A box was obtained. Merrick was brought up in a carriage with drawn blinds and was allowed to make use of the royal entrance so as to reach the box by a private stair. I had begged three of the hospital sisters to don evening dress and to sit in the front row in order to 'dress' the box, on the one hand, and to form a screen for Merrick on the other. Merrick and I occupied the back of the box which was kept in shadow. All went well, and no one saw a figure, more monstrous than any on the stage, mount the staircase or cross the corridor.

One has often witnessed the unconstrained delight of a child at its first pantomime, but Merrick's rapture was much more intense as well as much more solemn. Here was a being with the brain of a man, the fancies of a youth and the imagination of a child. His attitude was not so much that of delight as of wonder and amazement. He was awed. He was enthralled. The spectacle left him speechless, so that if he were spoken to he took no heed. He often seemed to be panting for breath. I could not help comparing him with a man of his own age in the stalls. This satiated individual was bored to distraction, would look wearily at the stage from time to time and then yawn as if he had not slept for nights; while at the same time Merrick was thrilled by a vision that was almost beyond his comprehension. Merrick talked of this pantomime for weeks and weeks. To him, as to a child with the faculty of make-believe, everything was real; the palace was the home of kings, the princess was of royal blood, the fairies were as undoubted as the children in the street, while the dishes at the banquet were of unquestionable gold. He did not like to discuss it as a play but rather as a vision of some actual world. When this mood possessed him he would say: 'I wonder what the prince did after we left,' or 'Do you think that poor man is still in the dungeon?' and so on and so on.

The splendour and display impressed him, but, I think, the ladies of the ballet took a still greater hold upon his fancy. He did not like the ogres and the giants, while the funny men impressed him as irreverent. Having no experience as a boy of romping and ragging, of practical jokes or of 'larks', he had little sympathy with the doings of the clown, but, I think (moved by some mischievous instinct in his subconscious mind), he was pleased when the policeman was smacked in the face, knocked down and generally rendered undignified.

Later on another longing stirred the depths of Merrick's mind. It was a desire to see the country, a desire to live in some green secluded spot and there learn something about flowers and the ways of animals and birds. The country as viewed from a wagon on a dusty high road was all the country he knew. He had never wandered among the fields nor followed the windings of a wood. He had never climbed to the brow of a breezy down. He had never gathered flowers in a meadow. Since so much of his reading dealt with country life he was possessed by the wish to see the wonders of that life himself.

This involved a difficulty greater than that presented by a visit to the theatre. The project was, however, made possible on this occasion also by the kindness and generosity of a lady – Lady Knightley – who offered Merrick a holiday home in a cottage on her estate. Merrick was conveyed to the railway station in the usual way, but as he could hardly venture to appear on the platform the railway authorities were good enough to run a second-class carriage into a distant siding. To this point Merrick was driven and was placed in the carriage unobserved. The carriage, with the curtains drawn, was then attached to the mainline train.

He duly arrived at the cottage, but the housewife (like the nurse at the hospital) had not been made clearly aware of the unfortunate man's appearance. Thus it happened that when Merrick presented himself his hostess, throwing her apron over her head, fled, gasping, to the fields. She affirmed that such a guest was beyond her powers of endurance, for, when she saw him, she was 'that took' as to be in danger of being permanently 'all of a tremble'.

Merrick was then conveyed to a gamekeeper's cottage which was hidden from view and was close to the margin of a wood. The man and his wife were able to tolerate his presence. They treated him with the greatest kindness, and with them he spent the one supreme holiday of his life. He could roam where he pleased. He met no one on his wanderings, for the wood was preserved and denied to all but the gamekeeper and the forester.

There is no doubt that Merrick passed in this retreat the happiest time he had as yet experienced. He was alone in a land of wonders. The breath of the country passed over him like a healing wind. Into the silence of the wood the fearsome voice of the showman could never penetrate. No cruel eyes could peep at him through the friendly undergrowth. It seemed as if in this place of peace all stain had been wiped away from his sullied past. The Merrick who had once crouched terrified in the filthy shadows of a Mile End shop was now sitting in the sun, in a clearing among the trees, arranging a bunch of violets he had gathered.

His letters to me were the letters of a delighted and enthusiastic child. He gave an account of his trivial adventures, of the amazing things he had seen, and of the beautiful sounds he had heard. He had met with strange birds, had startled a hare from her form, had made friends with a fierce dog, and had watched the trout darting in a stream. He sent me some of the wild flowers he had picked. They were of the commonest and most familiar kind, but they were evidently regarded by him as rare and precious specimens.

He came back to London, to his quarters in Bedstead Square, much improved in health, pleased to be 'home' again and to be once more among his books, his treasures and his many friends.

Some six months after Merrick's return from the country he was found dead in bed. This was in April, 1890. He was lying on his back as if asleep, and had evidently died suddenly and without a struggle, since not even the coverlet of the bed was disturbed. The method of his death was peculiar. So large and so heavy was his head that he could not sleep lying down. When he assumed the recumbent position the massive skull was inclined to drop backwards, with the result that he experienced no little distress. The attitude he was compelled to assume when he slept was very strange. He sat up in bed with his back supported by pillows, his knees were drawn up, and his arms clasped round his legs, while his head rested on the points of his bent knees.

He often said to me that he wished he could lie down to sleep 'like other people'. I think on this last night he must, with some determination, have made the experiment. The pillow was soft, and the head, when placed on it, must have fallen backwards and caused a dislocation of the neck. Thus it came about that his death was due to the desire that had dominated his life – the pathetic but hopeless desire to he 'like other people'.

As a specimen of humanity, Merrick was ignoble and repulsive; but the spirit of Merrick, if it could be seen in the form of the living, would assume the figure of an upstanding and heroic man, smooth browed and clean of limb, and with eyes that flashed undaunted courage.

His tortured journey had come to an end. All the way he, like another, had borne on his back a burden almost too grievous to bear. He had been plunged into the Slough of Despond, but with manly steps had gained the farther shore. He had been made 'a spectacle to all men' in the heartless streets of Vanity Fair. He had been ill-treated and reviled and bespattered with the mud of Disdain. He had escaped the clutches of the Giant Despair, and at last had reached the 'Place of Deliverance', where 'his burden loosed from off his shoulders and fell from off his back, so that he saw it no more'.

From *The Times*, December 4, 1886

'THE ELEPHANT MAN'

To the Editor of *The Times*

Sir, – I am authorized to ask your powerful assistance in bringing to the note of the public the following most exceptional case. There is now in a little room off one of our attic wards a man named Joseph Merrick, aged about 27, a native of Leicester, so dreadful a sight that he is unable even to come out by daylight to the garden. He has been called 'the elephant man' on account of his terrible deformity. I will not shock your readers with any detailed description of his infirmities, but only one arm is available for work.

Some 18 months ago, Mr. Treves, one of the surgeons of the London Hospital, saw him as he was exhibited in a room off the Whitechapel-road. The poor fellow was then covered by an old curtain, endeavouring to warm himself over a brick which was heated by a lamp. As soon as a sufficient number of pennies had been collected by the manager at the door, poor Merrick threw off his curtain and exhibited himself in all his deformity. He and the manager went halves inthe net proceeds of his exhibition, until at last the police stopped the exhibition of his deformities as against public decency. Unable to earn his livelihood by exhibiting himself any longer in England, he as persuaded to go over to Belgium, where he was taken in hand by an Austrian, who acted as his manager. Merrick managed in this way to save a sum of nearly £50, but the police there too kept him moving on, so that his life was a miserable and hunted one. One day, however, when the Austrian saw that the exhibition was pretty well played out, he decamped with poor Merrick's hardly-saved capital of E50, and left him alone and absolutely destitute in a foreign country. Fortunately, however, he had something to pawn, by which he raised sufficient money to pay his passage back to England, for he felt that the only friend he had in the world was Mr. Treves, of the London Hospital. He therefore, though with much difficulty, made his way there, for at every station and landing-place the curious crowd so thronged and dogged his steps that it was not an easy matter for him to get about. When he reached the London Hospital he had only the clothes in which he stood. He has been taken in by our hospital, though there is, unfortunately, no hope of his cure, and the question now arises what is to be done with him in the future.

He has the greatest horror of the workhouse, nor is it possible, indeed, to send him into any place where he could not insure privacy, since his appearance is such that all shrink from him.

The Royal Hospital for Incurables and the British Home for Incurables both decline to take him in, even if sufficient funds were forthcoming to pay for him.

The police rightly prevent his being personally exhibited again; he cannot go out into the streets, as he is everywhere so mobbed that existence is impossible; he cannot, in justice to others, be put in the general ward of a workhouse, and from such, even if possible, he shrinks with the greatest horror; he ought not to be detained in our hospital (where he is occupying a private ward, and being treated with the greatest kindness – he says he has never before known in his life what quiet and rest were), since his case is incurable, and not suited, therefore, to our overcrowded general hospital; the incurable hospitals refuse to take him in even if we paid for him in full, and the difficult question therefore remains what is to be done for him.

Terrible though his appearance is, so terrible indeed that women and nervous persons fly in terror from the sight of him, and that he is debarred from seeking to earn his livelihood in any ordinary way, yet he is superior in intelligence, can read and write, is quiet, gentle, not to say even refined in his mind. He occupies his time in the hospital by making with his one available hand little cardboard models, which he sends to the matron, doctor, and those who have been kind him. Through all the miserable vicissitudes of his life he carried about a painting of his mother to show that she was a decent and presentable person, and as a memorial of the only one who was kind to him in life until he came under the care of the nursing staff of the London Hospital and the surgeon who has befriended him.

It is a case of singular affliction brought about through no fault of himself; he can but hope for quiet and privacy during a life which Mr. Treves assures me is not likely to be long.

Can any of your readers suggest to me some fitting place where he can be received? And then I feel sure that, when that is found, charitable people will come forward and enable me to provide him with such accommodation. In the meantime, though it is not the proper place for such an incurable case, the little room under the roof of our hospital and out of Cotton Ward supplies him with all he wants. The Master of the Temple on Advent Sunday preached an eloquent sermon on the subject of our Master's answer to the question, 'Who did sin, this man or his parents, that he was born blind?' showing how one of the Creator's objects in permitting men to be born to a life of hopeless and miserable -disability was that the works of God should be manifested in evoking the sympathy and kindly aid of those on whom such a heavy cross is not laid.

Some 76,000 patients a year pass through the doors of our hospital, but I have never before been authorized to invite public attention to any particular case, so it may well be believed that this case is exceptional.

Any communication about this should be addressed either to myself or to the secretary at the London Hospital.

I have the honour to be, Sir, yours obediently,

P.C. CARR GOMM,
Chairman London Hospital.
November 30

From *The Times*, April 16, 1890

To the Editor of *The Times*

Sir, – In November, 1886, you were kind enough to insert in *The Times* a letter from me drawing attention to the case of Joseph Merrick, known as 'the elephant man.' It was one of singular and exceptional misfortune; his physical deformities were of so appalling a character that he was debarred from earning his livelihood in any other way than by being exhibited to the gaze of the curious. This having been rightly interfered with by the police of this country, he was taken abroad by an Austrian adventurer, and exhibited at different places on the Continent; but one day his exhibitor, after stealing all the savings poor Merrick had carefully hoarded, decamped, leaving him destitute, friendless, and powerless in a foreign country.

With great difficulty he succeeded somehow or other in getting to the door of the London Hospital, where, through the kindness of one of our surgeons, he was sheltered for a time. The difficulty then arose as to his future; no incurable hospital would take him in, he had a horror of the workhouse, and no place where privacy was unattainable was to be thought of, while the rules and necessities of our general hospital forbade the fund and space, which are set apart solely for cure and healing, being utilized for the maintenance of a chronic case like this, however abnormal. In this dilemma, while deterred by common humanity from evicting him again into the open street, I wrote to you, and from that moment all difficulty vanished; the sympathy of many was aroused, and, although no other fitting refuge offered, a sufficient sum was placed at my disposal, apart from the funds of the hospital, to maintain him for what did not promise to be a prolonged life. As an exceptional case the committee agreed to allow him to remain in the hospital upon the annual payment of a sum equivalent to the average cost of an occupied bed.

Here, therefore, poor Merrick was enabled to pass the three and a half remaining years of his life in privacy an comfort. The authorities of the hospital, the medical staff, the chaplain, the sisters, and nurses united to alleviate as far as possible the misery of his existence, and he learnt to speak of his rooms at the hospital as his home. There he receive kindly visits from many, among them the highest in the land and his life was not without various interests and diversions he was a great reader and was well supplied with books through the kindness of a lady, one of the brightest ornaments of the theatrical profession, he was taught basket-making, and on more than one occasion he was taken to the play, which he witnessed from the seclusion of a private box.

He benefited much from the religious instruction of our chaplain, and Dr. Walsham How, then Bishop of Bedford, privately confirmed him, and he was able by waiting in the vestry to hear and take part in the chapel services. The present chaplain tells me that on this Easter day, only five days before his death, Merrick was twice thus attending the chapel services, and in the morning partook of the Holy Communion; and in the last conversation he had with him Merrick had expressed his feeling of deep gratitude for all that had been done for him here, and his acknowledgment of the mercy of God to him in bringing him to this place. Each year he much enjoyed a six weeks' outing in a quiet country cottage, but was always glad on his return to find himself. once more 'at home.' In spite of all this indulgence he was quiet and unassuming, very grateful for all that was done for him, and conformed himself readily to the restrictions which were necessary.

I have given these details, thinking that those who sent money to use for his support would like to know how their charity was applied. Last Friday afternoon, though apparently in his usual health, he quietly passed away in sleep.

I have left in my hands a small balance of the money which has been sent to me from time to time for his support, and this I now propose, after paying certain gratuities, to hand over to the general funds of the hospital. This course, I believe, will be consonant with the wishes of the contributors.

It was the courtesy of *The Times* in inserting my letter in 1886 that procured for this afflicted man a comfortable protection during the last years of a previously wretched existence, and I desire to take this opportunity of thankfully acknowledging it. I am, Sir, your obedient servant,

F. C. CARR GOMM.
House Committee Room, London Hospital
April 15.

APPENDIX TWO:
LOVE AMONG THE LIMBLESS: TOD BROWNING'S "FREAKS"

After Tod Browning's vast directorial success with Universal's *Dracula* (1931), MGM were desperate to capitalize on the moment and rushed through production on a film project of his which had been in development since1929: *Freaks*. It proved to be the ultimate collision of cinema and sideshow.

The film was based on a short story by Clarence A. Robbins, whose story "Three Freaks" had earlier provided the inspiration for Browning's *The Unholy Three* [see appendix three]. "Spurs" was an absurd, somewhat sadistic vignette concerning a circus midget who inherits great wealth and is accepted in marriage by the Junoesque bareback rider he is obsessed with. (The midget also rides in his act, but his mount is a wolfhound.) At their wedding feast she humiliates him in front of his peers, boasting she can carry him like a child from one end of France to the other. A year later she reappears, broken and aged. It seems that the midget has kept her to her word, renouncing his former steed in her favour and driving her with his spurs along country roads until she has indeed carried him the exact distance she boasted of.

Tod Browning with some of the cast of "Freaks"

Browning, in collaboration with main screenwriters Willis Goldbeck and Leon Gordon, kept the bones of this tale but went on to flesh them with an even more extreme tale of sexual humiliation and revenge, set in a harrowing milieu of circus freaks and their secret codes of honour. Once the script was completed, Browning set about holding auditions for 'actors' to populate this sideshow world. He ended up with the very cream of top-line show-freaks from carnivals around America; most 'self-mades' were rejected, and only the most outlandish of genuine human anomalies made the final cast[1].

From the outset it was clear that Browning's vision for *Freaks* was extreme; indeed it seems that many exceptionally nasty or grotesque scenes and dialogue had to be excised during shooting. Even the finished version apparently included much more 'hardcore' footage of the freaks themselves,

footage included for road show audiences but deemed too much to stomach for regular cinema viewers. Shooting took around 9 weeks, from October to December 1931, and was often fraught; regular film people objected to the presence of the freaks in the studio canteen, and there was also some hierarchical friction within the sideshow performers themselves. At one point, MGM executives even tried to shut the film down, while Browning kept the publicity machine rolling regardless, flooding an eager press with tales of hermetic freak colonies and bizarre rituals.

When the film was finally completed, early censor-board and press reactions were decidedly mixed. After various required cuts had been made (the New York State censor demanding some thirty minutes be removed), the film eventually opened across America from the early to middle part of 1932. A reviewer for one leading trade journal swiftly declared the film as "so loathsome that I am nauseated thinking about it. The producers give an excuse that these creatures are all in the circus, implying that the characterizations are not that out of keeping with the conditions that may be imagined as existing in a circus. But this does not give them the right to do with them what the picture does. It is not fit to be shown anywhere". *Herald Tribune* remarked that "Mr Browning has always been an expert in pathological morbidity, but after seeing *Freaks*, his other films seem like whimsical fairytales", while the *New York Times* added: "The difficulty is in telling whether the film should be shown at the Rialto Theater – where it opened yesterday – or in, say, the Medical Center." The *New Yorker* was kinder, calling the film "a little gem"; the *Motion Picture Herald* conceded "...the production is bold and novel in conception and execution", and Louella Parsons was surprisingly supportive, saying "For pure sensationalism, *Freaks* tops any picture yet produced... a weird nightmare... a picture so different the public will want to see it". For once, she was proved wrong. *Variety*, in its summary of the film's opening months, encapsulated the extremes of reaction it engendered: "Planned by Metro to be one of the sensation pictures of the season, *Freaks* failed to qualify in the sure-fire category and has been shown in most parts of the country with astonishingly variable results. In spots it has been a clean-up. In others it was merely misery."

"We didn't lie to you, folks," the fairground barker shouts inside the sideshow at the opening of *Freaks*. "We told you we had living, breathing monstrosities! But for an accident of birth, you might be as they are!" The audience shifts uneasily. "They did not ask to be brought into the world." Now the hustler moves the people forward. "Their code is a law unto themselves. Offend one – and you offend them all." He takes the crowd to the edge of an open pit, where something squats at the bottom. There is a scream, but we cannot see what is at the bottom of the pit. "She was once a beautiful woman," proclaims the barker. "She was once known as the Peacock of the Air..."

With that, the film dissolves to a shot of an artist on the trapeze – the beautiful Cleopatra. She is played by Olga Baclanova with an air of studied sleaze, blonde and stealthy and predatory. Watching her from below is the midget Hans, played by Harry Earles (the thuggish 'baby' from Browning's earlier film *The Unholy Three*). He is the epitome of the American hero, only he happens to be three feet tall. Yet his mannered playing and instinctive courtesy make him sure of winning the sympathy of the viewer during the events to come.

Cleopatra descends, and drops her cloak in front of him; he is too short to replace it on her shoulders. It is a moment of social embarrassment as great as the Stroheim sequence when the society lady drops her glove and a cloaked man fails to retrieve it, being later revealed as armless. Cleopatra laughs at Hans, then patronises him by kissing his cheek like a schoolboy, despite his assertion that "I'm a man".

Having established the core of his drama, Hans' hopeless infatuation with an unfeeling 'big' woman, Browning then introduces us to his real world of freaks, when he shows us a flock of pinheads and midgets, some of the 'family' of sideshow artists, being taken for a walk along a sunny lakeside by their 'mother', Madame Tetrallini. This kind matriarch is touchingly played by Rose Dionne, an actress from the Sarah Bernhardt troupe. She soon has to defend her misshapen charges passionately against the verbal assaults of a passing game-keeper, who describes them as 'horrible, twisted things, crawling and gliding'. They are not monsters, but children, she counters, and they each have their place in God's world. After this speech, the viewer begins to feel more than mere pity for the freaks. They are so unselfconscious and innocent, that we begin to feel equally protective towards them.

Browning soon unveils the full repertoire of his sideshow cast, imported from all over the USA. Among those prodigies we meet are the Hilton sisters (who would later appear in the film *Chained For Life*); the pretty Siamese twins Daisy and Violet, who bicker about the man one of them is to marry; five shy pinheads: the Snow Twins, Zip and Pip, and Schlitzie; a bearded lady (Olga Roderick), who is about to give birth to a (bearded?) baby; a skeleton man (Pete Robinson), who is the proud father; a merry, agile half-man called Johnny Eck, who moves about like a bird on his hands; a Living Torso, the 'Hindu' Prince Randian, who has only a trunk and head and wriggles along the ground like a caterpillar; a half-man half-woman named Josephine-Joseph, whose female side has fallen in love with the circus strongman, Hercules; two armless girls, Martha Morris and Frances O'Connor; Koo Koo, the bird-woman; the midget Frieda, played by Daisy Earles (Harry's sister); and several dwarfs, including Angelo Rossitto. We also meet Phroso the Clown (Wallace Ford), and his girl Venus (Leila Hyams), their only other 'normal' friends.

The freaks are worried by Hans becoming increasingly infatuated with Cleopatra. The midget is lending her money and even buying her

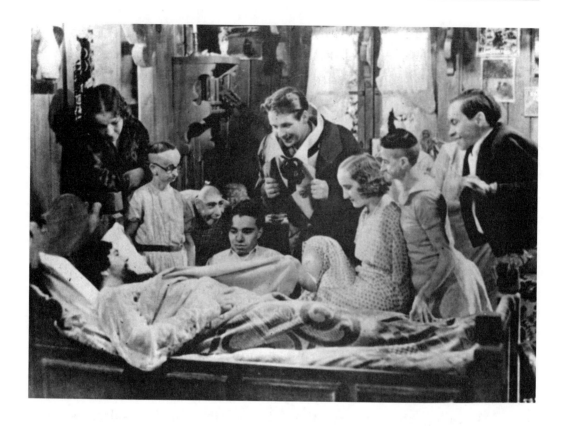

expensive gifts. As one of the dwarfs remarks, "Cleopatra isn't one of us. We're just filthy things to her." Still, she continues to take presents from Hans, leading him on, whilst secretly carrying on with her regular lover, the strongman Hercules. Hercules is equally calculating, and shrewd enough to realise that Hans' gifts, a platinum necklace, is worth thousands of dollars. The midget must be rich; he is worth exploiting. A plan begins to hatch...

Frieda, the tiny bareback rider who is in love with Hans, tries to reason with Cleopatra, pleading with her to release the hapless midget from her web. Frieda is all too aware that Cleopatra is only after the fortune which Hans has inherited, and inadvertently reveals the extent of his wealth. Cleopatra is merciless; she mocks Frieda, and drives her away. Then she settles down with Hercules, and they begin to plot in earnest. The only way to get the midget's fortune is for Cleopatra to marry him, and then get rid of him so that she and Hercules can enjoy the spoils together. They decide that this is the best course; after all, midgets are not strong, and can easily grow sick.

And so the great wedding-day approaches, and the freaks, desperate for Hans to be happy, have planned a special wedding feast to welcome Cleopatra to their ranks. A table is prepared in the big top, and so the scene is staged for Browning to produce the first of two stunning set-pieces: one of the most potent, memorable and alarming sequences in cinema, a grotesquerie still unequalled in cinema.

The festivities begin with sword-swallowers and fire-eaters, who perform as the freaks applaud. Cleopatra is seated at the head of the table, flanked by Hans and Hercules, quaffing liberal glasses of champagne. Soon she, and the freaks, are intoxicated. She grows more and more uninhibited, laughing at Hans' declarations of love and openly kissing her strongman lover, threatening to reveal her true colours; the freaks meanwhile work themselves into a tribalistic frenzy, beginning to thump on the table in accompaniment to the weird, strangulated wedding song they have devised

for Cleopatra: "Gooba gabba, gooba gabba, gooba gabba, one of us; gooba gabba, gooba gabba, gooba gabba, one of us; gooba gabba, we accept her, we accept her, one of us; gooba gabba, gooba gabba, we accept her, one of us!"

The limbless, the crawling, the crazed, all join in the refrain (sung in what director Browning would describe to the press as the "secret gibberish of the show-freaks") and sip in turn from the huge goblet of champagne carried by a dwarf who shuffles across the table (initial shots had him drooling into the cup). Finally, it is Cleopatra's turn to drink from the chalice, her time to be initiated into the ranks of the deformed. In a moment of drunken revelation she sees the full horror of her situation and, wracked with sudden revulsion, draws back and hurls the tainted champagne over her guests with a shriek of disgust:

"Freaks! Freaks! Dirty, filthy, stinking freaks!"

The assembly falls into stunned silence, then begins to scatter; Cleopatra picks up the comatose Hans, drapes him about her shoulders like a little boy, and exits followed by Hercules who blows a mocking farewell on his trumpet.

Weeks pass. Hans is growing inexplicably weaker and weaker, the doctor cannot find remedy; only Cleopatra can help him, nursing him and giving him his daily 'medicine'. But all the time, she is being watched. Dark shapes stir in the caravan shadow as she visits Hercules, perch on steps and sills overhearing them plot, peer from wagon windows as she administers the deadly medication.Hans, at first unbelieving, is finally alerted to the truth by his friends. Now it is their turn to conspire, to wreak revenge on the murderous lovers.

Hans surreptitiously stops taking the poison, while the others arm themselves with guns, knives and razors. Finally, the time for retribution is at hand. The carnival ups and moves on in the teeth of a midnight

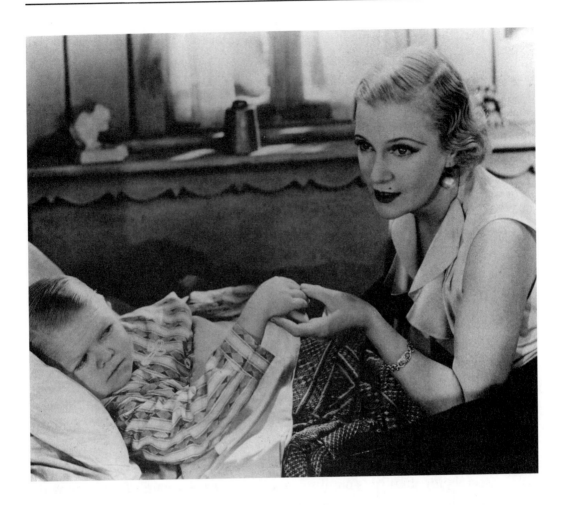

thunderstorm; we glimpse Johnny, running on his hands beneath Cleopatra's caravan. Just as she goes to give Hans more poison, his loyal friends appear from concealment. Just then the caravan hits a tree, splinters. Hercules comes to his shrieking lover's aid, freaks spilling out into the churning mud. As Cleopatra runs for safety, Hercules slips. He is surrounded by slithering, crawling, hopping shapes, their jagged weapons glinting in the lightning. Even Randian the human worm is there, a cut-throat razor clenched between his teeth.

Darkness descends upon the strongman's final scream... Next, Cleopatra is shown stumbling through a nearby wood. Like night-demons, the freaks are on her trail; then she too topples, pinned by a falling branch; the blades begin to flash once more. Blackout.

The film resumes where Browning first left off to tell his tale, with the barker at the geek-pit. His pitch continues: "...how she got that way will never be known. Some say a jealous lover. Others... the code of the freaks!"

At last, the freaks' handiwork is revealed. Cleopatra (barely recognizable) has been butchered and mutilated, truncated and disfigured; she is now nothing more than a squawking human chicken, shuffling and pecking at worms in the bone-pit. Not only has she become "one of us" to the freaks, she has become even less than they are, a true sub-human, the geek to end all geeks. The film fades on this startling image.

So ends *Freaks*, where Tod Browning's amputation/castration fixation had finally achieved delirium pitch. With Johnny Eck and Randian as his very own personal "evil mirror" eidolons, the director was able to give full rein to this bizarre fetish. Not content with the presence of these limbless protagonists, Browning makes it as implicit as possible that Hercules is ultimately emasculated in the mud; even the 'normal' Phroso implies his own impotence, quipping: "You should have caught me before my operation" to a female admirer. Sexual inadequacy and frustration (even perversion) underpin and drive the entire story. The Siamese twins gasp at the penetration of each other's lover; the hermaphrodite dreams of auto-copulation; Hans, with his infantile genitalia, can never consummate his Oedipal love for Cleopatra; jealousy and loss haunt the midway.

A creeping duality is omnipresent in *Freaks*. Although Browning wins our sympathy towards his twisted protagonists early on in the film, both the wedding-feast and the lightning-illuminated shots of them at the climax, slithering through the mud with vengeful intent, are truly shocking and re-establish an ambiguity toward their role; are they heroes or, ultimately, monsters? Is their dismemberment of Hercules and Cleopatra an act of righteous retribution, or in fact a resentful savagery perpetrated to bring these normal people down to their own level, to "cut them down to size"? Audiences seemed to think the latter, and many left the cinema screaming. This, coupled with poor reviews, proved disastrous. MGM panicked and withdrew the film, reputedly cutting a great deal of the more explicit footage before re-releasing it variously (and under the aegis of exploitation mogul Dwain Esper) as *Nature's Mistakes*, *Forbidden Love*, and *The Monster Show*. Lurid posters begged such dilemmas as: "Do Siamese Twins Make Love?"; "Can A Full Grown Woman Truly Love A Midget"; "Do The Pin-Heads

Think?"; and "What Sex Is The Half Man Half Woman?", while an apology was tacked on at the start of the film, assuring the viewer that ...the majority of freaks are endowed with normal thoughts and emotions... never again will such a story be filmed, as modern science and teratology is rapidly eliminating such blunders of nature from the world."

But even cuts, re-titling, and the addition of a moralistic prologue could not salvage Browning's maligned masterpiece. Seldom shown again in America and completely banned in England, *Freaks* was to prove the undoing of its maker. The outrage surrounding the film effectively finished Tod Browning's career; he made a few more films, including a last foray into the world of performers, *Miracles For Sale* (1932), but then faded into obscurity.

Freaks finally enjoyed a retrospective success, and new cult status, when fresh prints were circulated in the early '60s, the film being "re-discovered" by a successful showing at the Venice Film Festival of 1962 and gaining an eager new audience. It found instant acceptance amongst the New York underground film set, and played the midnight movie circuit there for years to come. *Freaks* was even allowed to be shown in England, after 30 years, where – thanks to the efforts of young film-maker Antony Balch – it ran at the Paris-Pullman in London, duly receiving such compliments as "Touching, funny and delicate" from the *Evening Standard*, and "Extraordinary! A plea for understanding" from the *Times*. Mindful perhaps of the thalidomide scandal, Nina Hibbin countered in the *Daily Worker*: "To release *Freaks* in the '60s, when misuse of science has produced its own appalling tragedies of deformation, I find hard to take"; but the film's new credibility was finally summed up by Penelope Gilliat in the *Observer*: "The film is moving, harsh, poetic, and genuinely tender. It triumphs at once over your nausea... What Browning has made is really a fable, concerned like most fables with pure ideas of trust and betrayal and revenge."

There is a final bitter irony to the story: Tod Browning, long-believed dead after his Hollywood career was cut short, was eventually found to be still living in 1962; yet he died from throat cancer, aged 80, on the 6th October that year, just a few months too soon to appreciate the rehabilitation of the film which had caused his earlier decline.

NOTES

1.   Very few other films have been made employing human anomalies as the main, or sole, players. These include the 1938 all-midget western *The Terror Of Tiny Town* and, most notably, Werner Herzog's horrific *Even Dwarves Started Small* (1970).

"Even Dwarves Started Small"

APPENDIX THREE:
"SPURS"
by
Tod Robbins

The inspiration for
Tod Browning's "Freaks"

I.

Jacques Courbé was a romanticist. He measured only twenty-eight inches from the soles of his diminutive feet to the crown of his head; but there were times, as he rode into the arena on his gallant charger, St. Eustache, when he felt himself a doughty knight of old about to do battle for his lady.

What matter that St. Eustache was not a gallant charger except in his master's imagination—not even a pony, indeed, but a large dog of a nondescript breed, with the long snout and upstanding aura of a wolf? What matter that M. Courbé's entrance was invariably greeted with shouts of derisive laughter and bombardments of banana skins and orange peel? What matter that he had no lady, and that his daring deeds were severely curtailed to a mimicry of the bareback riders who preceded him? What mattered all these things to the tiny man who lived in dreams, and who resolutely closed his shoe-button eyes to the drab realities of life?

The dwarf had no friends among the other freaks in Copo's Circus. They considered him ill-tempered and egotistical, and he loathed them for their acceptance of things as they were. Imagination was the armour that protected him from the curious glances of a cruel, gaping world, from the stinging lash of ridicule, from the bombardments of banana skins and orange peel. Without it, he must have shriveled up and died. But those others? Ah, they had no armour except their own thick hides! The door that opened on the kingdom of imagination was closed and locked to them; and although they did not wish to open this door, although they did not miss what lay beyond it, they resented and mistrusted any one who possessed the key.

Now it came about, after many humiliating performances in the arena, made palatable only by dreams, that love entered the circus tent and beckoned commandingly to M. Jacques Corbe. In an instant the dwarf was engulfed in a sea of wild, tumultuous passion.

Mlle. Jeanne Marie was a daring bareback rider. It made M. Jacques Courbé's tiny heart stand still to see her that first night of her appearance in the arena, performing brilliantly on the broad back of her aged mare, Sappho. A tall, blonde woman of the amazon type, she had round eyes of baby blue which held no spark of her avaricious peasant's soul, carmine lips and cheeks, large white teeth which flashed continually in a smile, and hands which, when doubled up, were nearly the size of the dwarf's head.

Her partner in the act was Simon Lafleur, the Romeo of the circus tent—a swarthy, hurculean young man with bold black eyes and hair that glistened with grease, like the back of Solon, the trained seal.

From the first performance, M. Jacques Courbé loved Mlle. Jeanne Marie. All his tiny body was shaken with longing for her. Her buxom charms, so generously revealed in tights and spangles, made him flush and cast down his eyes. The familiarities allowed to Simon Lafleur, the bodily acrobatic contacts of the two performers, made the dwarf's blood boil. Mounted on St. Eustache, awaiting his turn at the entrance, he would grind his teeth in impotent rage to see Simon circling round and round the ring, standing proudly on the back of Sappho and holding Mlle. Jeanne Marie in an ecstatic embrace, while she kicked one shapely, bespangled leg skyward.

"Ah, the dog!" M. Jacques Courbé would mutter. "Some day I shall teach this hulking stable boy his place! Ma foi, I will clip his ears for him!"

St. Eustache did not share his master's admiration for Mlle. Jeanne Marie. From the first he evinced his hearty detestation of her by low growls and a ferocious display of long, sharp fangs. It was little consolation for the dwarf to know that St. Eustache showed still more marked signs of rage when Simon Lafleur approached him. It pined M. Jacques Courbé to think that his gallant charger, his sole companion, his bedfellow, should not also love and admire the splendid giantess who each night risked life and limb before the awed populace. Often, when they were alone together, he would chide St. Eustache on his churlishness.

"Ah, you devil of a dog!" the dwarf would cry. "Why must you always growl and show your ugly teeth when the lovely Jeanne Marie condescends to notice you? Have you no feelings under your tough hide? Cur, she is an angel, and you snarl at her! Do you not remember how I found you, starving puppy in a Paris gutter? And now you must threaten the hand of my princess! So this is you gratitude, great hairy pig!"

M. Jacques Courbé had one living relative—not a dwarf, like himself, but a fine figure of a man, a prosperous farmer living just outside the town of Roubaix. The elder Courbé had never married; and so one day, when he was found dead from heart failure, his tiny nephew—for whom, it must be conversion—fell heir to a comfortable property. When the tidings were brought to him, the dwarf threw both arms about the shaggy neck of St. Eustache and cried out:

"Ah, now we can retire, marry and settle down, old friend! I am worth many times my weight in gold!"

That evening as Mlle. Jeanne Marie was changing her gaudy costume after the performance, a light tap sounded on the door.

"Enter!" she called, believing it to be Simon Lafleur, who had promised to take her that evening to the Sign of the Wild Boar for a glass of wine to wash the sawdust out of her throat. "Enter, mon Cheri!"

The door swung slowly open; and in stepped M. Jacques Courbé, very proud and upright, in the silks and laces of a courtier, with a tiny gold-hilted sword swinging at his hip. Up he came, his shoe-button eyes all a-glitter to see the more than partially revealed charms of his robust lady. Up he came to within a yard of where she sat; and down on one knee he went and pressed his lips to her red-slippered foot.

"Oh, most beautiful and daring lady," he cried, in a voice as shrill as a pin scratching on a window pane, "will you not take mercy on the unfortunate Jacques Courbé? He is hungry for your smiles, he is starving for you lips! All night long he tosses on his couch and dreams of Jeanne Marie!"

"What play acting is this, my brave little fellow?" she asked, bending down with the smile of an ogress. "Has Simon Lafleur sent you to tease me?"

"May the black plague have Simon!" the dwarf cried, his eyes seeming to flash blue sparks. "I am not play acting. It is only too true that I love you, mademoiselle; that I wish to make you my lady. And now that I have a fortune, not that—" He broke off suddenly, and his face resembled a withered apple, "What is this, mademoiselle?" he said, in the low, droning tone of a hornet about to sting. "Do you laugh at my love? I warn you, mademoiselle— do not laugh at Jacques Courbé!"

Mlle. Jeanne Marie's large, florid face had turned purple from suppressed merriment. Her lips twitched at the corners. It was all she could do not to burst out into a roar of laughter.

Why, this ridiculous little manikin was serious in his love-making! This pocket-sized edition of a courtier was proposing marriage to her! He, this splinter of a fellow, wished to make her his wife! Why, she could carry him about on her shoulder like a trained marmoset!

What a joke this was—what a colossal, corset-creaking joke! Wait till she told Simon Lafleur! She could fairly see him throw back his sleek head, open his mouth to its widest dimensions, and shake with silent laughter. But she must not laugh—not now. First she must listen to everything the dwarf had to say; draw all the sweetness of this bonbon of humour before she crushed it under the heel of ridicule.

"I am not laughing," she managed to say. "You have taken me by surprise. I never thought, I never even guessed—"

"That is well, mademoiselle," the dwarf broke in. "I do not tolerate laughter. In the arena I am paid to make laughter; but these others pay to laugh at me. I always make people pay to laugh at me!"

"But do I understand you aright, M. Courbé? Are you proposing an honourable marriage?"

The dwarf rested his hand on his heart and bowed. "Yes, mademoiselle, and honourable, and the wherewithal to keep the wolf from the door. A week ago my uncle died and left me a large estate. We shall have a servant to wait on our wants, a horse and carriage, food and wine of the best, and leisure to amuse ourselves. And you? Why, you will be a fine lady! I will clothe that beautiful big body of yours with silks and laces! You will be as happy, mademoiselle, as a cherry tree in June!"

Jeanne Marie accepts Courbé's proposal. This concept from the story is reflected in this Freaks publicity still, although it was not used in the script or the film.

The dark blood slowly receded from Mlle. Jeanne Marie's full cheeks, her lips no longer twitched at the corners, her eyes had narrowed slightly. She had been a bareback rider for years, and she was weary of it. The life of the circus tent had lost its tinsel. She loved the dashing Simon Lafleur; but she knew well enough that this Romeo in tights would never espouse a dowerless girl.

The dwarf's words had woven themselves into a rich mental tapestry. She saw herself a proud lady, ruling over a country estate, and later welcoming Simon Lafleur with all the luxuries that were so near his heart. Simon would be overjoyed to marry into a country estate. These pygmies were a puny lot. They died young! She would do nothing to hasten the end of Jacques Courbé. No, she would be kindness itself to the poor little fellow; but, on the other hand, she would not lose her beauty mourning for him.

"Nothing that you wish shall be withheld from you as long as you love me, mademoiselle," the dwarf continued. "Your answer?"

Mlle. Jeanne Marie bent forward, and with a single movement of her powerful arms, raised M. Jacques Courbé and placed him on her knee. For an ecstatic instant she held him thus, as if he were a large French doll, with his tiny sword cocked coquettishly out behind. Then she planted on his cheek a huge kiss that covered his entire face from chin to brow.

"I am yours!" she murmured, pressing him to her ample bosom. "From the first I loved you, M. Jacques Courbé!"

II.

The wedding of Mlle. Jeanne Marie was celebrated in the town of Roubaix, where Copo's Circus had taken up its temporary quarters. Following the ceremony, a feast was served in one of the tents, which was attended by a whole galaxy of celebrities.

The bridegroom, his dark little face flushed with happiness and wine, sat at the head of the board. His chin was just above the tablecloth, so that his head looked like a large orange that had rolled off the fruit dish. Immediately beneath his dangling feet, St. Eustache, who had more than once evinced by deep growls his disapproval of the proceedings, now worried a bone with quick, sly glances from time to time at the plump legs of his new mistress. Papa Copo was on the dwarf's right, his large round face as red and benevolent as a harvest moon. Next to his sat Griffo, the giraffe boy, who was covered with spots and whose neck was so long that he looked down on all the rest, including M. Hercule Hippo the giant. The rest of the company included Mlle. Lupa, who had sharp white teeth of a incredible length and who growled when she tried to talk; the tiresome M. Jegongle, who insisted on juggling fruit, plates and knives, although the whole company was heartily sick of his tricks; Mme. Samson, with her trained boa constrictors coiled about her neck and peeping out timidly, one above each ear; Simon Lafleur, and a score of others.

The bareback rider had laughed silently and almost continually ever since Jeanne Marie had told him of her engagement. Now he sat next to her in his crimson tights. His black hair was brushed back from his forehead and so glistened with grease that it reflected the lights overhead, like a burnished helmet. From time to time, he tossed off a brimming goblet of burgundy, nudged the bride in the ribs with his elbow, and threw back his sleek head in another silent outburst of laughter.

"And you are sure you will not forget me, Simon?" she whispered. "It may be some time before I can get the little ape's money."

"Forget you, Jeanne?" he muttered. "By all the dancing devils in champagne, never! I will wait as patiently as Job till you have fed that mouse some poisoned cheese. But what will you do with him in the meantime, Jeanne? You must allow him some liberties. I grind my teeth to think of you in his arms!"

The bride smiled, and regarded her diminutive husband with an appraising glance. What an atom of a man! And yet life might linger in his bones for a long time to come. M. Jacques Courbé had allowed himself only one glass of wine, and yet he was far gone in intoxication. His tiny face was suffused with blood, and he stared at Simon Lafleur belligerently. Did he suspect the truth?

"Your husband is flushed with wine!" the bareback rider whispered. "Ma foi, madame, later he may knock you about! Possibly he is a dangerous fellow in his cups. Should he maltreat you, Jeanne, do no forget that you have a protector in Simon Lafleur."

"You clown!" Jeanne Marie rolled her large eyes roguishly, and laid her hand for an instant on the bareback rider's knee. "Simon, I could crack his skull between my finger and thumb, like a hickory nut!" She paused to illustrate her example, and then added reflectively: "And, perhaps, I shall do that very thing, if he attempts any familiarities. Ugh! The little ape turns my stomach!"

By now the wedding guests were beginning to show the effects of their potations. This was especially marked in the case of M. Jacques Courbé's associates in the side-show.

Griffo, the giraffe boy, had closed his large brown eyes, and was swaying his small head languidly above the assembly, while a slightly supercilious expression drew his lips down at the corners. M. Hercule Hippo, swollen out by his libations to even more colossal proportions, was repeating over and over: "I tell you I am not like other men. When I walk, the earth trembles!" Mlle. Lupa, her hairy upper lip lifted above her long white teeth, was gnawing at a bone, growling unintelligible phrases to herself and shooting savage, suspicious glances at her companions. M. Jejongle's hands had grown unsteady, and as he insisted on juggling the knives and plates of each new course, broken bits of crockery littered the floor. Mme. Samson, uncoiling her necklace of baby boa constrictors, was feeding them lumps of sugar soaked in rum. M. Jacques Courbé had finished his second glass of wine, and was surveying the whispering Simon Lafleur through narrowed eyes.

There can be no genial companionship among great egotists who have drunk too much. Each one of these human oddities thought that he or she was responsible for the crowds that daily gathered at Copo's Circus; so now, heated with the good Burgundy, they were not slow in asserting themselves. Their separate egos rattled angrily together, like so many pebbles in a bag . Here was gunpowder which needed only a spark.

"I am a big—a very big man!" M. Hercule Hippo said sleepily. "Women love me. The pretty little creatures leave their pygmy husbands, so that they may come and stare at Hercule Hippo of Copo's Circus. Ha, and when they return home, they laugh at other men always! 'You may kiss me again when you grow up,' they tell their sweethearts."

"Fat bullock, here is one woman who has no love for you!" cried Mlle. Lupa, glaring sidewise at the giant over her bone. "That great carcass of yours is only so much food gone to waste. You have cheated the butcher, my friend. Fool, women do not come to see you! As well might they stare at the cattle being let through the street. Ah, no, they come from far and near to see one of their own sex who is not a cat!"

"Quite right," cried Papa Copo in a conciliatory tone, smiling and rubbing his hands together. "Not a cat, mademoiselle, but a wolf. Ah, you have a sense of humor! How droll!"

"I have a sense of humor," Mlle. Lupa agreed, returning to her bone, "and also sharp teeth. Let the erring hand not stray too near!"

"You, M. Hippo and Mlle. Lupa, are both wrong," said a voice which seemed to come from the roof. "Surely it is none other than me whom the people come to stare at!"

All raised their eyes to the supercilious face of Griffo, the giraffe boy, which swayed slowly from side to side on its long, pipe stem neck. It was he who had spoken, although his eyes were still closed.

"Of all the colossal impedance!" cried the matronly Mme. Samson. "As if my little dears had nothing to say on the subject!" She picked up the two baby boa constrictors, which lay in drunken slumber on her lap, and shook them like whips at the wedding guests. "Papa Copo knows only too well that it is on account of these little charmers, Mark Antony and Cleopatra, that the side-show is so well-attended!"

The circus owner, thus directly appealed to, frowned in perplexity. He felt himself in a quandary. These freaks of his were difficult to handle. Why had he been fool enough to come to M. Jacques Courbé's wedding feast? Whatever he said would be used against him.

As Papa Copo hesitated, his round, red face wreathed in ingratiating smiles, the long deferred spark suddenly alighted in the powder. It all came about on account of the carelessness of M. Jejongle, who had become engrossed in the conversation and wished to put in a word for himself. Absent-mindedly juggling two heavy plates and a spoon, he said in a petulant tone:

"You all appear to forget me!"

Scarcely were the words out of his mouth, when one of the heavy plates descended with a crash on the thick skull of M. Hippo; and M. Jejongle was instantly remembered. Indeed he was more than remembered; for the giant, already irritated to the boiling point by Mlle. Lupa's insults, at the new affront struck out savagely past her and knocked the juggler head-over-heels under the table.

Mlle. Lupa, always quick-tempered and especially so when her attention was focused on a juicy chicken bone, evidently considered her dinner companion's conduct far from decorous, and promptly inserted her sharp teeth in the offending hand that had administered the blow. M. Hippo, squealing from rage and pain like a wounded elephant, bounded to this feet, overturning the table.

Pandemonium followed. Every freak's hands, teeth, feet, were turned against the others. Above the shouts, screams, growls, and hisses of the combat, Papa Copo's voice could be heard bellowing for peace.

"Ah, my children, my children! This is no way to behave! Calm yourselves, I pray you! Mlle. Lupa, remember that you are a lady as well as a wolf!"

There is no doubt that M. Jacques Courbé would have suffered most in this undignified fracas, had it not been for St. Eustache, who had stationed himself over his tiny master and who now drove off all would be assailants. As it was, Griffo, the unfortunate giraffe boy, was the most defenseless and therefore became the victim. His small, round head swayed back and forth to blows like a punching bag. He was bitten by Mlle. Lupa, buffeted by M. Hippo, kicked by M. Jejongle, clawed by Mme. Samson, and nearly strangled by both of the baby boa constrictors which had wound themselves about his neck like hangmen's nooses. Undoubtedly be would have fallen a victim to circumstances, had it not been for Simon Lafleur, the bride and half a dozen of her acrobatic friends, whom Papa Copo had implored to restore peace. Roaring with laughter, they sprang forward and tore the combatants apart.

M. Jacques Corbe was found sitting grimly under a fold of tablecloth. He held a broken bottle of wine in one hand. The dwarf was very drunk, and in a towering rage. As Simon Lafleur approached with one of his silent laughs, M. Jacques Courbé hurled the bottle at his bead.

"Ah, the little wasp!" the bareback rider cried, picking up the dwarf by his waistband. "Here is your fine husband, Jeanne! Take him away before he does me some mischief. Parbleu, he is a bloodthirsty fellow in his cups!"

The bride approached, her blonde face crimson from wine and laughter. Now that she was safely married to a country estate, she took no more pains to conceal her true feelings.

"Oh, la, la!" she cried, seizing the struggling dwarf and holding him forcibly on her shoulder. "What a temper the little ape has! Well, we shall spank it out of him before long!"

"Let me down!" M. Jacques Courbé screamed in a paroxysm of fury. "You will regret this, madame! Let me down, I say!"

The horsey-back ride appears in Freaks, but as a much more minor event than it is to become in Spurs.

But the stalwart bride shook her head. "No, no, my little one!" she laughed. "You cannot escape your wife so easily! What, you would fly from my arms before the honeymoon!"

"Let me down!" he cried again. "Can't you see that they are laughing at me!"

"And why should they not laugh, my little ape? Let them laugh, if they will; but I will not put you down. No, I will carry you thus, perched on my shoulder, to the farm. It will set a precedent which brides of the future may find a certain difficulty in following!"

"But the farm is quite a distance from here, my Jeanne," said Simon Lafleur. "You are strong as an ox, and he is only a marmoset; still I will wager a bottle of Burgundy that you set him down by the roadside."

"Done, Simon!" the bride cried, which a flash of her strong white teeth. "You shall lose your wager, for I swear that I could carry my little ape from one end of France to the other!"

M. Jacques Courbé no longer struggled. He now sat bolt upright on his brides broad shoulder. From the flaming peaks of blind passion, he had fallen into an abyss of cold fury. His love was dead, but some quite alien emotion was rearing an evil head from its ashes.

"Come!" cried the bride suddenly. "I am off. Do you and the others, Simon, follow to see me win my wager."

They all trooped out of the tent. A full moon rode the heavens and showed the road, lying as white and straight through the meadows as the parting in Simon Lafleur's black, oily hair. The bride, still holding the diminutive bridegroom on her shoulder, burst out into song as she strode forward. The wedding guests followed. Some walked none too steadily. Griffo, the giraffe boy, staggered pitifully on his long, thin legs. Papa Copo alone remained behind.

"What a strange world!" he muttered, standing in the tent door and following them with his round blue eyes. "Ah, there children of mine are difficult at times—very difficult!"

III.

A year had rolled by since the marriage of Mlle. Jeanne Marie and M. Jacques Courbé. Copo's Circus had once more taken up its quarters in the town of Roubaix. For more than a week the country people for miles around had flocked to the side-show to get a peep at Griffo, the giraffe boy; M. Hercule Hippo, the giant; Mlle. Lupa, the wolf lady; Mme. Samson, with her baby boa constrictors; and M. Jejongle, the famous juggler. Each was still firmly convinced that he or she alone was responsible for the popularity of the circus.

Simon Lafleur sat in his lodgings at the Sign of the Wild Boar. He wore nothing but red tights. His powerful torso, stripped to the waist, glistened with oil. He was kneading his biceps tenderly with some strong-smelling fluid.

Suddenly there came the sound of heavy, laborious footsteps on the stairs. Simon Lafleur looked up. His rather gloomy expression lifted, giving place to the brilliant smile that had won for him the hearts of so many lady acrobats.

"Ah, this is Marcelle!" he told himself. "Or perhaps it is Rose, the English girl; or, yet again, little Francesca, although she walks more lightly. Well no matter—whoever it is, I will welcome her!"

By now, the lagging, heavy footfalls were in the hall; and, a moment later, they came to a halt outside the door. There was a timid knock.

Simon Lafleur's brilliant smile broadened. "Perhaps some new admirer that needs encouragement," he told himself. But aloud he said, "Enter, mademoiselle!"

The door swung slowly open and revealed the visitor. She was a tall, gaunt woman dressed like a peasant. The wind had blown her hair into her eyes. Now she raised a large, toil-worn hand, brushed it back across her forehead and looked long and attentively at the bareback rider.

"Do you not remember me?" she said at length.

Two lines of perplexity appeared above Simon Lafleur's Roman nose; he slowly shook his head. He, who had known so many women in his time, and now at a loss. Was it a fair question to ask a man who was no longer a boy and who had lived? Women change so in a brief time! Now this bag of bones might at one time have appeared desirable to him.

Parbleu! Fate was a conjurer! She waved her wand; and beautiful women were transformed into hogs, jewels into pebbles, silks and laces into hempen cords. The brave fellow, who danced to-night at the prince's ball, might to-morrow dance more lightly on the gallows tree. The thing was to live and die with a full belly. To digest all that one could—that was life!

"You do not remember me?" she said again.

Simon Lafleur once more shook his sleek, black head. "I have a poor memory for faces, madame," he said politely. "It is my misfortune, when there are such beautiful faces."

"Ah, but you should have remembered, Simon!" the woman cried, a sob rising in her throat. "We were very close together, you and I. Do you not remember Jeanne Marie?"

"Jeanne Marie!" the bareback rider cried. "Jeanne Marie, who married a marmoset and a country estate? Don't tell me. Madame, that you—"

He broke off and stared at her, open-mouthed. His sharp black eyes wandered from the wisps of wet, straggling hair down her gaunt person till they rested at last on her thick cowhide boots incrusted with layer on layer of mud from the countryside.

"It is impossible!" he said at last.

"It is indeed Jeanne Marie," the woman answered, "or what is left of her. Ah, Simon, what a life he has led me! I have been merely a beast of burden! There are no ignominities which he has not made me suffer!"

"To whom do you refer?" Simon Lafleur demanded. "Surely you cannot mean that pocket edition husband of yours—that dwarf, Jacques Courbé?"

"Ah, but I do, Simon! Alas, he has broken me!"

"He—that toothpick of a man?" the bareback rider cried, with one of his silent laughs. "Why, it is impossible! As you once said yourself, Jeanne, you could crack his skull between finger and thumb like a hickory nut!"

"So I thought once. Ah, but I did not know him then, Simon! Because he was small, I thought I could do with him as I liked. It seemed to me that I was marrying a manikin. 'I will play Punch and Judy with this little fellow,' I said to myself. Simon, you imagine my surprise when he began playing Punch and Judy with me!"

"But I do not understand, Jeanne. Surely at any time you could have slapped him into obedience!"

"Perhaps," she assented wearily, "had it not been for St. Eustache.

From the first that wolf dog of his hated me. If I so much as answered his master back, he would show his teeth. Once, at the beginning when I raised my hand to cuff Jacques Corbe, he sprang at my throat and would have torn me limb from limb, had the dwarf not called him off. I was a strong woman, but even then I was no match for a wolf!"

"There was poison, was there not?" Simon Lafleur suggested.

"Ah, yes, I, too, thought of poison; but it was of no avail. St. Eustache would eat nothing that I gave him; and the dwarf forced me to taste first of all food that was placed before him and his dog. Unless I myself wished to die, there was no way of poisoning either of them."

"My poor girl!" the bareback rider said, pityingly. "I begin to understand; but sit down and tell me everything. This is a revelation to me, after seeing you stalking homeward so triumphantly with your bridegroom on you shoulder. You must begin at the beginning."

"It was just because I carried him thus on my shoulder that I have had to suffer so cruelly," she said, seating herself on the only other chair the room afforded. "He has never forgiven me the insult which he says I put upon him. Do you remember how I boasted that I could carry him from one end of France to the other?"

"I remember. Well, Jeanne?"

"Well, Simon, the little demon has figured out the exact distance in leagues. Each morning, rain or shine, we sully out of the house—he on my back, and the wolf dog at my heels—and I tramp along the dusty roads till my knees tremble beneath me from fatigue. If I so much as slacken my pace, if I falter, he goads me with cruel little golden spurs; while, at the same time, St. Eustache nips my ankles. When we return home, he strikes so many leagues of a score which he says is the number of leagues from one end of France to the other. Not half that distance has been covered, and I am no longer a strong woman, Simon. Look at these shoes!"

She held up one of her feet for his inspection. The sole of the cowhide boot had been worn through; Simon Lafleur caught a glimpse of bruised flesh caked with the mire of the highway.

"This is the third pair that I have had," she continued hoarsely. "Now he tells me that the price of shoe leather is too high, that I shall have to finish my pilgrimage barefooted."

"But why do you put up with all this, Jeanne?" Simon Lafleur asked angrily. "You, who have a carriage and a servant, should not walk at all!"

"At first there was a carriage and a servant," she said, wiping the tears from her eyes with the back of her hand, "but they did not last a week. He sent the servant about his business and sold the carriage at a near-by fair. Now there is no one but me to wait on him and his dog."

"But the neighbours?" Simon Lafleur persisted. "Surely you could appeal to them?"

"We have no neighbours; the farm is quite isolated. I would have run away many months ago, if I could have escaped unnoticed; but they keep a continual watch on me. Once I tried, but I hadn't traveled more than a league before the wolf dog was snapping at my ankles. He drove me back to the farm, and the following day I was compelled to carry the little fiend until I fell from sheer exhaustion."

"But to-night you got away?"

"Yes," she said, and with a quick, frightened glance at the door. "To-night I slipped out while they were both sleeping, and came here to you. I know that you would protect me, Simon, because of what we have been to each other. Get Papa Copo to take me back in the circus, and I will work my fingers to the bone! Save me, Simon!"

Jeanne Marie could longer suppress her sobs. They rose in her throat, choking her, making her incapable of further speech.

"Calm yourself, Jeanne," Simon Lafleur told her soothingly. "I will do what I can for you. I shall discuss the matter with Papa Copo to-morrow. Of course, you are no longer the woman that you were a year ago. You have aged since then, but perhaps our good Papa Cope could find you something to do."

He broke off and eyed her intently. She had sat up in the chair; her face, even under its coat of grime, had turned a sickly white.

"What troubles you, Jeanne?" he asked a trifle breathlessly.

"Hush!" she said, with a finger to her lips. "Listen!"

Simon Lafleur could hear nothing but the tapping of the rain on the roof and the sighing of the wind through the tree. An unusual silence seemed to pervade the Sign of the Wild Boar.

"Now don't you hear it?" she cried with an in articulate gasp. "Simon, it is in the house—it is on the stairs!"

At last the bareback rider's less sensitive ears caught the sound his companion had heard a full minute before. It was a steady pit-pat, pit-pat, on the stairs, hard to dissociate from the drop of the rain from the eaves; but each instant it came nearer, grew more distinct.

"Oh, save me, Simon; save me!" Jeanne Marie cried, throwing herself at his feet and clasping him about his knees. "Save me! It is St. Eustache!"

"Nonsense, woman!" the bareback rider said angrily, but nevertheless he rose. "There are other dogs in the world. On the second landing, there is a blind fellow who owns a dog Perhaps that is what you hear."

"No, no—it is St. Eustache's step! My God, if you had lived with him a year, you would know it, too! Close the door and lock it!"

"That I will not," Simon Lafleur said contemptuously. "Do you think I am frightened so easily? If it is the wolf dog, so much the worse for him. He will not be the first cur I have choked to death with these two hands!"

Pit-pat, pit-pat—it was on the second landing. Pit-pat, pit-pat—now it was in the corridor, and coming fast. Pit-pat—all at once it stopped.

There was a moment's breathless silence, and then into the room trotted St . Eustache. M. Jacques sat astride the dog's broad back, as he had so often done in the circus ring. He held a tiny drawn sword; his shoe-button eyes seemed to reflect its steely glitter.

The dwarf brought the dog to a halt in the middle of the room, and took in, at a single glance, the prostrate figure of Jeanne Marie. St. Eustache, too, seemed to take silent note of it. The stiff hair on his back rose up, he showed his long white fangs hungrily, and his eyes glowed like two live coals.

"So I find you thus, madame!" M. Jacques Courbé said at last. "It is fortunate that I have a charger here who can scent out my enemies as well as hunt them down in the open. Without him, I might have had some difficulty in discovering you. Well, the little game is up. I find you with your lover!"

"Simon Lafleur is not my lover!" she sobbed. "I have not seen him once since I married you until to-night! I swear it!"

"Once is enough," the dwarf said grimly. "The imprudent stable boy must be chastised!"

"Oh, spare him!" Jeanne Marie implored. "Do not harm him, I beg of you! It is not his fault that I came! I—"

But at this point Simon Lafleur drowned her out in a roar of laughter.

"Ha, ha!" he roared, putting his hands on his hips. "You would chastise me, eh? Nom d'un chien! Don't try your circus tricks on me! Why, hope-o'-my-thumb, you who ride on a dog's back like a flea, out of this room before I squash you. Begone, melt, fade away!" He paused, expanded his barrel-like chest, puffed out his cheeks, and blew a great breath at the dwarf. "Blow away, insect," he bellowed, "lest I put my heel on you!"

M. Jacques Corbe was unmoved by this torrent of abuse. He sat very upright on St. Eustache's back, his tiny sword resting on his tiny shoulder.

"Are you done?" he said at last, when the bareback rider had run dry of invectives. "Very well, monsieur! Prepare to receive cavalry!" He paused for an instant, then added in a high clear voice: "Get him, St. Eustache!"

The dog crouched, and at almost the same moment, sprang at Simon Lafleur. The bareback rider had no time to avoid him and his tiny rider. Almost instantaneously the three of them had come to death grips. It was a gory business.

Simon Lafleur, strong man as he was, was bowled over by the dog's unexpected leap. St. Eustache's clashing jaws closed on his right arm and crushed it to the bone. A moment later the dwarf, still clinging to his dog's back, thrust the point of his tiny sword into the body of the prostrate bareback rider.

Simon Lafleur struggled valiantly, but to no purpose. Now he felt the fetid breath of the dog fanning his neck, and the wasp-like sting of the dwarf's blade, which this time found a mortal spot. A convulsive tremor shook him and he rolled over on his back. The circus Romeo was dead.

M. Jacques Corbe cleansed his sword on a kerchief of lace, dismounted, and approached Jeanne Marie. She was still crouching on the floor, her eyes closed, her head held tightly between both hands. The dwarf touched her imperiously on the broad shoulder which had so often carried him.

"Madame," he said, "we now can return home. You must be more careful hereafter. Ma foi, it is an ungentlemanly business cutting the throats of stable boys!"

She rose to her feet, like a large trained animal at the word of command.

"Do you wish to be carried?" she said between livid lips.

"Ah, that is true, madame," he murmured. "I was forgetting our little wager. Ah, yes! Well, you are to be congratulated, madame—you have covered nearly half the distance."

"Nearly half the distance," she repeated in a lifeless voice.

"Yes, madame," M. Jacques Courbé continued. "I fancy that you will be quite a docile wife by the time you have done." He paused, and then added reflectively: "It is truly remarkable how speedily one can ride the devil out of a woman—with spurs!"

* * * * * * *

Papa Copo had been spending a convivial evening at the Sign of the Wild Boar. As he stepped out into the street, he saw three familiar figures preceeding him—a tall woman, a tiny man, and a large dog with upstanding ears. The woman carried the man on her shoulder; the dog trotted at her heels.

The circus owner came to a halt and stared after them. His round eyes were full of childish astonishment.

"Can it be?" he murmured. "Yes, it is! Three old friends! And so Jeanne carries him! Ah, but she should not poke fun at M. Jacques Courbé! He is so sensitive; but, alas, they are the kind that are always hen-pecked!"

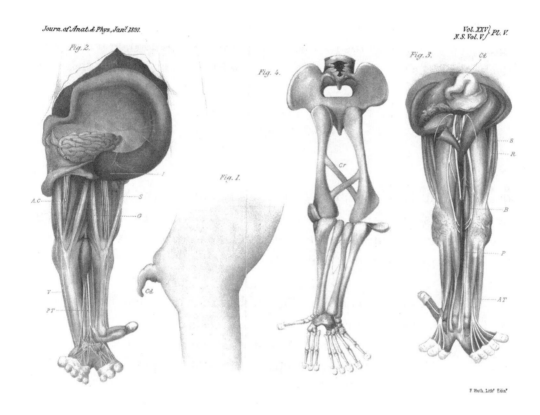

Journ. of Anat. & Phys., Jan.ʸ 1891.

Vol. XXV } *Pl. V.*
N.S. Vol. V.

F. Huth, Lith.ʳ Edin.ʳ

Fig.1. Profile of undissected foetus, showing caudal appendage and absence of external genitals.

Fig. 2. Anterior view of semi-dissected foetus, showing terminations of intestine, rotation of limbs, plantar surfaces of feet, position of muscles, and distribution of arteries and nerves.

Fig. 3. Posterior view, showing position of caudal appendage; left gluteus maximus cut; small and great sciatic nerves, with primary division of latter; one large median artery; anterior aspect of leg and dorsal surface of feet.

Fig. 4. Posterior view of skeleton, showing pelvic outlet; fusion of tuberosities of ischia and pubic rami; position of acetabula; crucial muscle; rotation of lower limb and fusion of the two ossa calcis and cuboid and external cuneiform: absence of left middle cuneiform; Cd, caudal appendage; I, dilated end of intestine; S, sartorius; G, gracilis; R, rectus; B, biceps; P, peroneus longus; cr, crucial muscle; AT, anterior tibial artery and nerve; PT, posterior tibial artery and nerve; V, vein.

APPENDIX FOUR:
"THE DISSECTION OF A SYMELIAN MONSTER"
by
R C Benington

A True Account
first published in 1891

SYMELIAN monsters are of sufficient rarity to make a specimen one of interest. Reports of authentic cases are difficult to find. Palfyn, in his work on "Monstrosities," mentions a child without feet, having its thighs joined, and ending in a sort of point, date 1553. But no attempt is made at an anatomical description.

The family is characterised, as the name implies, by a union more or less complete of the lower limbs, and the classification adopted by Geoffrey St Hilaire[1] is based upon the extent of union, and the existence or absence of various bones or toes.

1. Symelic, in which the two lower limbs are united, are very complete – two feet with the soles turned to the front.

2. Uromelic, in which the two lower limbs are united but are incomplete, the limb containing sometimes three bones, sometimes two, and only one patella. The foot is usually very incomplete in the number of bones-either tarsal, metatarsal, or phalanges. In this class of foetus there is neither anus nor urinary passages. The internal sexual organs are wanting on either one or both sides; when present are usually male. The external organs are frequently present. Two cases of this kind are reported as having been born alive. One lived nine hours and swallowed a little pap.

3. Sirens, in which the two lower limbs are united, are very incomplete, ending in a point, without a distinct foot, or the foot being represented by a toe or rudiment of a toe. In a case described by Hofer,[2] there is behind the segment resulting from union of lower limbs a tail-like appendage, less long than the segment, soft, vascular, spongy, and without muscular fibres, obtuse at its extremity, inserted like an animal's tail, just above the anal orifice.

Superville[2] also describes a Siren, in which a little pig-like tail was inserted above the anus on the middle of sacrum. The terminal segment usually consists of one bone, analogous to the tibia. This form is more common than the others. In them, out of twelve reported cases three were females, one male; in nine, the organs were too rudimentary for differentiation, or were absent. The intestines are badly formed in the post-caecal region. The end of the colon and rectum are wanting. These have been
born alive at full term, and have lived from six to twenty-four hours, one executing various movements, cried, and swallowed.

St Hilaire describes to some extent the anatomical peculiarities of a Symelic foetus,and his descriptiont allies well with those observed by myself in the following:–

The child was born at full term. Above the pelvis it was well developed and perfect.

The lower limbs were united from the pelvis downwards. There were two feet, with the soles turned anteriorly, but only nine toes, the second toe of the left foot being absent. The left big toe was almost at right angles to its normal position, and long, having much the appearance of the similar toe of an ape.

There was an entire absence of external genito-urinary organs, and no sign of an anus.

In the position indicated in fig. 1 was a pig-like caudal appendage. Above this the spinal column ended in a truncated extremity directed backwards.

On opening the thorax the conditions found were normal. The lungs were small, and occupied only the back part of the thoracic cavity. They were of a light reddish-brown colour, and sank in water. On opening the abdomen nothing abnormal was found until reaching the caecum. Above this point the intestine was enlarged, filled with meconium, and the sigmoid flexure ended in a blunted cone. The spleen and liver were normal. The supra-renal bodies were present and large. The kidneys, ureters, and bladder were entirely wanting. The testicles were in the inguinal region. There was only one umbilical artery.

Most of these features will be seen on fig. 2, which also shows the position of the limbs. They will be seen to be turned outwards, so that the patellae are placed externally and posteriorly.

The tibioe and fibulae have a greater degree of rotation than the femora. The fibulae are both present, near to each other in the middle line. In consequence of this rotation, the muscles seen above the knee are more or less normal, consisting of the adductors, sartorius and gracilis, whilst below the knee the normally posterior muscles are anterior. They are the flexor longus hallucis, flexor longus digitorum, and tibialis posticus.

Internally, above the knee, are seen two muscular strips passing upwards and outwards between the adjacent surfaces of the femora. In the middle line is a muscle which I take to represent the gastrocnemius. The small femoral arteries are seen to end in the patellar plexus.

There is only one posterior tibial artery which supplies the plantar aspect of both feet. In this diagram also are seen a few branches of the antero-crural nerve and two posterior tibial nerves-the larger, the right, supplying the plantar surfaces of both feet; the smaller, the left, going to the big toe of that side. The fuller development of the right limb will also be noted.

On dissecting the back the tail was found to be surrounded by muscular fibres which emerged from the pelvis, of which further detail is given below.

Fig. 3 is a posterior view with the left gluteus maximus cut. It shows above the knee the following muscles:–

Tensor fasciae, rectus and vasti, and sartorius externally. Below the knee, the four internal tendons are the peronei, then the extensor longus digitorum, extensor hallucis, and tibialis anticus.

Internally, at the level of the knee-joint and above, are seen the two femoral heads of the biceps and a median slip all continuous with the peroneus longus. The great and small sciatic nerves and a large median artery are seen to emerge from the pelvic outlet. The union of the two great sciatic nerves into one median popliteal, and two external popliteal is also shown. In the leg are seen the anterior tibial arteries and nerves.

The following muscles were found, and were normal in their attachments:–

Psoas, iliacus, tensor fascie, sartorius, gracilis, rectus femoris, vasti, pectineus, adductors brevis and longus, gluteus maximus and minimus, obturator externus, tibialis anticus, extensor longus digitorum, extensor hallucis, peroneus brevis, flexor longus hallucis, flexor longus digitorum, tibialis posticus, extensor brevis digitorum.

The following deviations were noted:–

The adductor magnus came too far down; it appeared to become continuous with the posterior ligament of the knee-joint, and was attached to the back of the tibia,in the position of the normal semi-membranosus. The popliteus was very immature; only a few indistinct muscular fibres indicated its position.

The Gluteus Mledius.–

The posterior fibres of this muscle, opposite the part corresponding to the great sacro-sciatic opening, passed into the pelvis, where they intermingled with others of intra-pelvic origin, and invested the tail in both its intra- and extra-pelvic portions.

Nothing corresponding to the semi-membranosus, or semi-tendinosus, or long head of biceps could be found. The femoral head of each biceps was normal, and the two muscles passed downwards, and at the space between the condyles of the femora and above they were separated from each other by a muscular mass, which was clearly defined from them. Below, the biceps and
this median mass passed imperceptibly into the peroneus longus. They seemed to be attached to a fibrous aponeurosis from the upper part of the condyle of the femur to some distance below the head of the fibula.

Taking origin from the anterior side of this aponeurosis on both sides,and therefore being connected to the back of both condyles of the femora, was a fleshy mass two centimetres long and five wide, ending abruptly in a fine tendon, which, passing downwards, was attached to the inner and back part of the internal malleolus of right tibia; this I have taken to represent the gastrocnemius and tendo Achillis. There was nothing to represent the soleus.

Stretching between the femora were two muscular slips arising from the adjacent borders, and, passing downwards and inwards, to be inserted along the adjacent surfaces of the opposite femora, thus forming a crucial muscle, the one having its highest attachment to the left femur being anterior
(fig. 4).

On opening a hip-joint the appearances were normal. On opening the right knee-joint itwas seen that the synovial membrane passed from the femur, immediately below the patella facet to blend with the infra-patellar pad of fat, thus representing a broad ligamentum mucosum. In this way the joint between patella and femur was lined by a synovial membrane, distinct from that of the general joint cavity, except that there was a continuity between the two synovial cavities over the front of external condyle. Both semi-lunar cartilages were present. No transverse ligament connecting them anteriorly could be made out. Both crucial ligaments were present.

The great trochanters were closely approximated and held together by a dense fibrous structure.

In the lower limb there are three interosseous membranes: one between the two fibula and one between each fibula and tibia. The lower end of each fibula is very large, and resembles the inferior extremity of the radius. The internal malleolus is on a much lower level than the external.

Tarsal Bones.–

There is one large os calcis to which both fibulae are articulated. There is evidence that they have been two separate bones, as a groove can be detected between them.

On the right foot, the astragalus articulates with tibia, fibula, os calcis, and scaphoid.

On the left foot with tibia and scaphoid. The other tarsal bones are all present in right foot, and apparently normal, as also the metatarsal.

On the left side, there is an absence of the middle cuneiform, and a corresponding absence of second toe. The cuboid and external cuneiform are both present, but fused. The sacrum is nearly at a right angle with the lumbar vertebrae; the number of sacral vertebrae is normal. The ilia are flattened out in a marked manner; this flattening is accompanied by a close approximation of the tuberosities of the ischia, so that they are united; the acetabula being thus carried backwards, their cavities look almost directly backwards. The corresponding approximation of the pubes has resulted in a complete fusion of the ischial and pubic rami. The obturator membranes thereby form, as it were, part of the floor of the pelvis, the obturator foramina looking directly downwards. The brim of the pelvis is markedly elongated from before backwards; there is no pelvic cavity, so to speak, but a space corresponding to the inferior strait is left between the sacral angle and the united ischia, measuring two centimetres transversely, and seven antero-posteriorly. The lower end of femur has made about a quarter turn, the tibia half a turn, so that their posterior surfaces have become anterior.

At the lower border of the last lumbar vertebrae, the abdominal aorta gave off one large median artery and four lateral branches. The large median branch passed backwards and made its exit from the pelvis, accompanied by the great sciatic nerves through the inferior strait. It passed down the back of the thigh, and at the level of the knee it divided into three: one posterior and two anterior tibial arteries. The two anterior tibials preserved their normal relations to muscles and nerves. The posterior tibial passed down the anterior surface of the leg, as seen in fig. 2, and was the main source of the blood-supply to both feet. Of the lateral branches arising from the abdominal aorta, two were external and two internal iliacs. The femorals were very small and indistinct, but could be traced down to the patella, where they ended in the patellar plexus.

The internal iliacs were not traced.

The two great sciatic nerves (fig. 3) united to form a large median trunk, which passed down the leg and divided into two, one of which, the larger, supplied both feet (plantar surfaces); the other, much smaller, only the left big toe (fig. 2). The external popliteals divided in normal situation into muscular cutaneous and anterior tibials, the distribution of which appeared normal.

The caudal appendage, which had been cut off externally for microscopical examination, was traced inwards. It was found to become invested by muscular fibres derived from the gluteus medius and intra-pelvic fibres, and to extend upwards 2X5 centimetres, in size about the thickness of a goose-quill. It ended abruptly opposite the last lumbar vertebrae, and was densely surrounded by connective tissue, nerves, and blood-vessels. It was placed in the median line – in front of the termination of the aorta and body of sacrum. On section, it showed a minute canal, which just admitted a bristle.

The history of the case was given to me as follows:–

Mother has had three children, perfect; all alive and well. Mother's age, 38. Both she and her husband not deformed in any way, and no history of such in other branches of family.

Full time child.

Mother says, three months ago, whilst carrying the child, she was kicked in the abdomen by the husband, which laid her up for three weeks.

I am indebted to Professor Windle, of Queen's College, Birmingham, for the following account of the microscopical appearances of the specimens submitted to him:-

"The caudal appendage is composed almost entirely of muscular tissue, chiefly arranged longitudinally, but in part consisting of transversely lying bundles. It contains an artery of some size, which runs longitudinally through it, and which, from the position occupied by the appendage, was probably the termination of the middle sacral artery.

"Another longitudinally running tube of considerable size is a vein. The nature of this was at first a little doubtful, but careful examination settled the question. There is no evidence of the presence of cartilaginous nodules in the appendage, and it certainly contains no pieces of bone. I have looked through all the chief Teratological works, but can find no account of any sireniform foetus with a similar appendage. In an account of a Dicephalus tripus dibrachius given by Becker[3] there is mention made of a 2 cm. long 1 cm. broad, tail-like process, which over-hung the funnel-shaped opening which represented the anus. This appendage consisted of connective tissue with vessels. Ecker and His[4] have discussed the question of the presence of a caudal appendage in the human embryo, and the paper of the former author is illustrated with sections of the tail end of foetuses at various ages. There is an account of the same condition in Sutton's *Evolution and Disease*.[5] I should think the specimen in question is undoubtedly one of these caudal appendages or skin tails. The muscular fibres, which do not appear to penetrate to its most distal part, would in this case represent the muscles of the tail, curvatores caudis, etc., representatives of which are at times met with in the human subject.

"The other section appears to be undoubtedly suprarenal capsule."

NOTES

1. *Histoire des Anomalies, ou Traité de Teratologie*, vol. ii., 1836.
2. Quoted by St Hilaire, p. 252, vol. ii.
3. "'Dissertation,'" Göttingen; Abst. in *Virchow u. Hirsch. Jahresabericht Jahrg.*, xvi., vol. i. p. 271.
4. *Arch. für Anat. u. Phys.*, (Anat. abth.), 1880.
5. Pp. 52, *et seq.*